NEHEMIAH

REBUILDING HOPE IN OUR LIVES AND OUR NATION

BIBLE STUDY AND REFLECTIONS

By

KAREN L. DWYER, PHD

AND

LAWRENCE A. DWYER, JD

Joy of the Lord is Your Strength

(Nehemiah 8:10)

Nehemiah: Rebuilding Hope in Our Lives and Our Nation
Bible Study and Reflections

KLD Books, Inc.
Omaha, Nebraska

ISBN: **13: 978-0-9992061-6-4**
ISBN-10: 0999206168

For additional information, other titles, or speaking, email: **kldbooksomaha@gmail.com**

Original printing 2011
Second Edition, 2017

Scriptures quotations are from USCCB approved translations, as noted:

Cover Design by Hannah Reynolds, Omaha.

Cover Picture. *Nehemiah Makes His Petition to Artaxerxes* by Scottish Painter William Brassey Hole (c. 1925). This Painting shows Nehemiah, the cupbearer, making his petition to King Artaxerxes. United States Public Domain.[i]

Published in the United States of America

DEDICATION

TO OUR PRECIOUS FRIENDS IN THE

HEART OF JESUS PRAYER GROUP

AND

MARTIN'S BIBLE STUDY

Table of Contents

THE INTRODUCTION

Connection Question

Have you ever lived far away from home and longed to return to your roots and family?

Welcome to Persia 445 BC!

Nehemiah: Rebuilding Hope and Faith in Our Lives and Our Nation is a fourteen-lesson study about the power of prayer and a nation's turning back to God that changed everything in the lives of a broken and destitute people. It began with a man named Nehemiah, who was broken-hearted over the condition of his people and his homeland. He wept. He prayed and fasted. He repented and sought God. Then God answered him. By God's great grace and favor, Nehemiah inspired a discouraged people to join him in rebuilding their nation.

The Book of Nehemiah speaks to our faith today, even though it was written almost 2500 years ago. It can inspire us in a time when the people of God are discouraged, in trouble, embattled and even obstinate in the struggle with a culture conflicted with God's ways. Nehemiah reminds us how God's presence and power are with us and that God will guide us in rebuilding our spiritual lives and encouraging those around us. Today, just as he did for Nehemiah, God calls us to prayer, trust and surrender. He longs to be the center of our lives. He desires to strengthen us with His power and presence so that we have the courage, fortitude and direction to work together to receive His healing and to rebuild the brokenness in our lives and our nation.

The Book of Nehemiah is set during the reign **Artaxerxes I,** King of the Persian Empire (464 to 424 BC.). In 605 BC, Babylonian **King Nebuchadnezzar** took the Jewish people into captivity at a time when they had been unfaithful to God and His commands. In 535 BC, after 70 years in captivity and the overthrow of Babylon, Persian **King Cyrus** allowed the Jews led by Zerubbabel (Ezra 6: 6-12) to return to Jerusalem to rebuild their Temple. It was a very hard time for the people of God because their enemies harassed them and hired counselors (i.e., lawyers) to speak against them during every step of the rebuilding. After Cyrus, the next kings stopped all rebuilding efforts until **King Darius** allowed them to complete the temple around 515 BC. In 478 BC, during the reign of King **Ahasuerus** (also called Xerxes, 486 - 465 BC), Esther and Mordecai through God's providential hand, helped save the nation of Israel from annihilation. **The Book of Nehemiah follows the time after Esther**

In 458 BC, **King Artaxerxes I**, the son of **Ahasuerus (Xerxes I)** and likely the stepson of Esther[ii], allowed Ezra and the priests, Levites, singers, gatekeepers, and temple servants to return to Jerusalem (Ezra 7: 11-26) to refurbish their temple and make offerings. But the city was still in ruins by 445 BC, the people were disheartened and all of the city gates were burned down. THIS IS TIME WHERE WE MEET NEHEMIAH.

The Book of Nehemiah is a historical book in the Old Testament detailing the third return of the God's people from the Babylonian captivity, dating about 445 BC. It is a memoir written by Nehemiah to clearly demonstrate how God intervened when the nation returned to Him. The change depended on God's people who repented, interceded and rededicated themselves to follow God and His Word in everything. The repentance and commitment led to great joy, celebration and a renewal of faith that changed the direction of a nation and many lives.

God had a purpose for Nehemiah and the book offers a message for our generation, outlining the importance of: 1) praising God and declaring His greatness 2) interceding for your nation and your family, 3) working and praying arm-in-arm against wickedness, 4) encouraging others in the faith, 5) being faithful in following God and closing down the gates where evil enters your life, 6) seeking God in all things and 7) leading with passion. This book will reassure you that prayer changes everything, that every obstacle can be overcome, and that every false accusation or persecution can lead to prayer and victorious persistence, even in the most difficult challenges. God is with us. He is at work. He has a plan that changes everything!

Nehemiah is most of all a book of inspiration and hope! Nehemiah reminds us: *The joy of the LORD will be your strength* (Nehemiah 8: 10). That means you will be able to say, *I can do ALL things through Christ who strengthens me* (Philippians 4: 13).

Within this study, you will find

CONNECTIONS. Each chapter starts with a *Connection* to help you prayerfully connect the events of your life with the events in Nehemiah's life, some 2500 years ago.

SCRIPTURES FROM THE BOOK OF NEHEMIAH. Each chapter in this study contains the actual Scripture passages of the Book of Nehemiah from the New Revised Standard Version-Catholic Edition translation (NRSVCE), approved by the United States Conference of Catholic Bishops and used by permission from the National Council of the Churches of Christ in the United States of America.

QUESTIONS. Study Questions follow the *Connections*. The questions are grouped by themes to help you focus on the verses, follow the events and understand their significance.

NOTES. Definitions of difficult terms are included to explain the meaning of words in Scripture that may not be familiar to readers today. In addition, historical notes are offered to provide background.

PONDERINGS. Some questions include *Ponderings*—based on Luke 1:29 where Mary *pondered* the meaning of the Word of the Lord. These ponderings add personal reflection and meditation on the meaning of the verses.

COMMENTARY. Commentary can be found among the questions. It will provide cultural context, perspective, themes and summaries.

REFLECTIONS AND APPLICATION. Each chapter includes *Reflections* on principles from the Scriptures studied, and to encourage personal *Application*.

PERSONAL PRAYER RESPONSE. Each chapter ends with a *Personal Prayer Response* that invites you to respond with a heartfelt prayer to the Lord, asking His help in your life based on the Scriptures read in each chapter.

TIPS FOR SMALL GROUP STUDY. See the *Appendix* for information on how to facilitate a small group study using this book.

1

NEHEMIAH AND JERUSALEM

Connection Question

Do you have unfinished projects that will trouble you until you get them done?

Nehemiah Prays and Weeps[iii]
St. Takla.Org
Nehemiah prays and weeps before of the Lord
Nehemiah 1: 4-11

Chapter One - Nehemiah and Jerusalem

A Historical Book

The Book of Nehemiah is a historical book. It was one of the last books written in the Old Testament, with events starting around 445 BC.[iv] In Hebrew, the book was originally joined to the Book of Ezra to form one continuous story. In the Greek translation of the Bible (i.e., the Septuagint), the Book of Ezra was broken into two parts, entitled *1 and 2 Esdras.* By the third century, the two parts were called Ezra and Nehemiah. Thus, Nehemiah became the thirteenth book of the Old Testament, where we still find it today.[v]

Nehemiah was the author of this book, although some Jewish historians attribute the book to Ezra. As you read Chapters 1-7 and 12-13, it becomes obvious that Nehemiah likely wrote most of the book because of the first-person narration. Actually, the chapters sound like a collection of his notes that could be called "Nehemiah's Memoirs." However, Chapters 8, 9 and 10 seem like they could have been written by Ezra and inserted at a different time.

As the book opens, Nehemiah is living in Persia and longs to hear about his family and homeland in Jerusalem. Judah had been broken down by Babylonian invasions, starting about 605 BC and continuing until 586 BC when all of Judah, Jerusalem, and the Temple were completely destroyed by King Nebuchadnezzar. Many of the people and best of everything were carried away to Babylon. (This time of exile from Israel beginning about 605 BC is called the Babylonian captivity.)

In 538 BC, under the leadership of Zerubbabel, and with the support of Persian King Cyrus, some Jews returned to Jerusalem to rebuild their Temple, which was completed in 515 BC. This rebuilding eventually ceased because the returnees were harassed and oppressed by the surrounding peoples. In 458 BC, King Artaxerxes allowed Ezra to return to Jerusalem to refurbish the temple and make offerings, but the city still was in ruins and suffered even more attacks.

In 445 BC, we meet Nehemiah who has a high position in the court of King Artaxerxes at Susa in Persia. His heart is dedicated to the Lord. When he hears of devastating troubles in Jerusalem, he weeps, repents, fasts and seeks the Lord with fervent prayer. Then using his God-given position, he obtains help from the king to rebuild his broken homeland. From the beginning of Chapter 1, Nehemiah demonstrates to us how to rebuild the brokenness in our lives through fervent prayer, a love and dedication to the Word of God, a compassion for people, a courageous faith, and a deep conviction that inspires others when they need all the encouragement they can get.

Chapter One Questions

1. ***NEHEMIAH 1.*** In preparation for this study, please read Nehemiah 1 *below* and **circle** the verse(s) about Nehemiah that get your attention. Then share why these verses caught your attention.

Nehemiah 1

The words of Nehemiah the son of Hacaliah. Now it happened in the month of Chislev, in the twentieth year, as I was in Susa the capital, 2 one of my brothers, Hanani, came with certain men from Judah; and I asked them about the Jews that survived, those who had escaped the captivity, and about Jerusalem. 3 They replied, "The survivors there in the province who escaped captivity are in great trouble and shame; the wall of Jerusalem is broken down, and its gates have been destroyed by fire."

4 When I heard these words I sat down and wept, and mourned for days; fasting and praying before the God of heaven. 5 I said, "O LORD God of heaven, the great and awesome God who keeps covenant and steadfast love with those who love him and keep his commandments; 6 let your ear be attentive and your eyes open to hear the prayer of your servant that I now pray before you day and night for your servants, the people of Israel, confessing the sins of the people of Israel, which we have sinned against you. Both I and my family have sinned. 7 We have offended you deeply, failing to keep the commandments, the statutes, and the ordinances that you commanded your servant Moses. 8 Remember the word that you commanded your servant Moses, 'If you are unfaithful, I will scatter you among the peoples; 9 but if you return to me and keep my commandments and do them, though your outcasts are under the farthest skies, I will gather them from there and bring them to the place at which I have chosen to establish my name.' 10 They are your servants and your people, whom your redeemed by your great power and by your strong

hand. 11 O Lord, let your ear be attentive to the prayer of your servant, and to the prayer of your servants who delight in revering your name. Give success to your servant today, and grant him mercy in the sight of this man." At the time, I was cupbearer to the king. NRSVCE

Notes. *Nehemiah* (v. 1) in Hebrew means "the Lord comforts."[vi]
Chislev (v. 1) on the Hebrew calendar is November-December in 445 BC.
The twentieth year (v. 1) refers to the year in the reign of Artaxerxes I.[vii]
Susa (v. 1), was the principle capital of the Persian Empire and the winter residence of King Artaxerxes.
Hanani (v. 2) is a shortened form of Hananiah and means "the Lord is gracious." [viii]
Brother (e.g., of Hanani, v. 2) in Hebrew is pronounced "awkn" and can mean brother of the same parents, half-brother, relative, countryman or kinsman.

2. ***NEHEMIAH AND JERUSALEM.*** According to v. 1-3 and 11, record in the following space what you learned about Nehemiah and his homeland?

WHAT I LEARNED ABOUT NEHEMIAH AND HIS SITUATION...

a. Who is narrating the story? (v. 1)

b. Where is Nehemiah living (v. 1)

c. Who came to visit Nehemiah in Susa (v. 2)?

d. What is the problem that Nehemiah hears (v. 3)?

e. What was Nehemiah's occupation (v. 11)?

Note. _A cupbearer_ *(v. 11)* was a high-ranking officer who served wine to the king at his royal table. The King feared plots and intrigues with the possibility he could be poisoned from the food or wine. Thus, the cupbearer was close to the king as he tasted everything before it entered the king's mouth. He had to be a man of irreproachable loyalty, who had the complete confidence of the king. The position was highly valued and one of esteem and influence in the culture.

3. ***NEHEMIAH WEEPS.*** How did Nehemiah respond to the bad news (v. 4)?

Note. *To mourn* (v. 4) means to grieve beyond the usual feelings of sadness. It implies an internal weeping of someone who is deeply affected. *To weep* implies the physical release of tears in time of sadness. Nehemiah both "wept and mourned for days."

❖Ponderings

a. Why would Nehemiah have such an emotional response about the problem so far away in Jerusalem?

b. On a personal note, list the things that break your heart today.

- something in your personal life,
- something concerning a member of your family or a close friend, or
- something happening in our country?

Nehemiah Weeps

Nehemiah was the cupbearer to Artaxerxes, the great king of Persia—who ruled over 127 provinces from the border of China on the east to the Mediterranean on the west. This was a very high position in the kingdom because it was the cupbearer who tasted every morsel or drop of wine before the king could consume it. (If the cupbearer dropped dead or would not eat in fear of poisoning from the king's enemies, the king would know not to eat it either!) It was a close position to the king; the king depended on him, trusted him and would likely talk with him often. One day when Nehemiah was going about his life as usual, his kinsman and others arrived from Judah. Nehemiah was obviously happy to see Hanani and hear the news of his family and friends who were still living in the homeland so he quickly inquired about Jerusalem. The report was bad news, "The survivors there in the province who escaped exile are in great trouble and shame; the wall of Jerusalem is broken down, and its gates are destroyed by fire." When Nehemiah heard these words, he became greatly disturbed and wrote, "I sat down and wept, and mourned for days; and I continued fasting and praying before the God of heaven."

Now we have a first impression of Nehemiah. He is a man of status, a Godly and compassionate man. He is a man of prayer. Although he could have continued to enjoy the delectable palace wine and food that he tasted everyday with the king, in his grief he turned to God. In fasting and prayer, he cried out to God with intercessions on behalf of his broken brethren and homeland over 500 miles away in Jerusalem.

4. ***<u>SUFFERINGS.</u>*** In order to understand why Nehemiah would care about the troubles in Jerusalem—so many miles away, please read the following Old Testament verses. Then circle all the sufferings and troubles the people of Jerusalem experienced.

2 Chronicles 36: 14-23. All the leading priests and the people also were exceedingly
unfaithful, following all the abominations of the nations; and they polluted the
house of the Lord that he had consecrated in Jerusalem. 15 The LORD, the God of their
fathers, sent persistently to them by his messengers, because he had compassion on
his people and on his dwelling place; 16 but they kept mocking the messengers of
God, despising his words, and scoffing at his prophets, till the wrath of the LORD
rose against his people, till there was no remedy. 17 Therefore he brought up against
them the king of the Chaldeans, who slew their young men with the sword in the
house of their sanctuary, and had no compassion on young man or virgin, old man
or aged; he gave them all into his hand. 18 And all the vessels of the house of God,

great and small, and the treasures of the house of the LORD, and the treasures of the king and of his princes, all these he brought to Babylon. [19] And they burned the house of God, and broke down the wall of Jerusalem, and burned all its palaces with fire, and destroyed all its precious vessels. [20] He took into exile in Babylon those who had escaped from the sword, and they became servants to him and to his sons until the establishment of the kingdom of Persia, [21] to fulfill the word of the LORD by the mouth of Jeremiah, until the land had enjoyed its Sabbaths." NRSVCE

2 Kings 25: 10-12. And all the army of the Chaldeans, who were with the captain of the guard, broke down the walls around Jerusalem. [11] And the rest of the people who were left in the city and the deserters who had deserted to the king of Babylon,* together with the rest of the multitude, Nebuzaradan the captain of the guard carried into exile. [12] But the captain of the guard left some of the poorest of the land to be vinedressers and plowmen. NRSVCE

Ezra 4: 3- 22. But Zerubbabel, Jeshua, and the rest of the heads of families in Israel said to them, "You shall have no part with us in building a house to our God; but we alone will build to the Lord, the God of Israel, as King Cyrus of Persia has commanded us." [4] Then the people of the land **discouraged the people of Judah**, and **made them afraid to build**, [5] and they bribed officials to **frustrate their plan** throughout the reign of King Cyrus of Persia and until the reign of King Darius of Persia. [7] And in the days of Artaxerxes, Bishlam and Mithredath and Tabeel and the rest of their associates wrote to King Artaxerxes of Persia… "To King Artaxerxes: Your servants, the people of the province Beyond the River, send greeting. And now [12] may it be known to the king that the Jews who came up from you to us have gone to Jerusalem. They are rebuilding that rebellious and **wicked city**; they are finishing the walls and repairing the foundations. [13] Now may it be known to the king that, if this city is rebuilt and the walls finished, they will **not pay tribute, custom, or** toll, and the royal revenue will be reduced. ... [16] We make known to the king that, if this city is rebuilt and its walls finished, you will then have **no possession in the province** Beyond the River."
[17] The king sent an answer: "... [21] Therefore issue an order that **these people be made to cease, and that this city not be rebuilt, until I make a decree**. [22] Moreover, take care not to be slack in this matter; why should damage grow to the hurt of the king?" NRSVCE

***Note.** Nebuchadnezzar is also called in Scripture the *King of the Chaldeans* or the *King of Babylon*.

5. ***TROUBLES.*** Based on what you circled in the last question, what **events** led to the destruction of Jerusalem by the Babylonians?

❖Ponderings

a. **Troubles to the people.** How damaging to the people was the invasion of Jerusalem?

b. **Troubles rebuilding.** Even when they tried to rebuild the Temple, what happened (Ezra 4)?

6. ***THE IMPORTANCE OF JERUSALEM.*** Read the following Historical and Biblical Timeline and the Chart of Jerusalem. Then circle what you find interesting about the importance of Jerusalem in Biblical history.

Historical and Biblical Timeline of Jerusalem[ix]

Genesis 14: 17-20. Jerusalem was first called **Salem**, which means peace. ("And Melchizedek king of Salem brought out bread and wine; he was the priest of God Most High, **initiating the priesthood**. [19] ...And he blessed Abram...

Genesis 22: 2-4. Abraham was commanded by God to sacrifice his son Isaac at the Hill of Moriah in Jerusalem.

1 Chronicles 11: 3-5. About 1050 BC, David was anointed King and immediately captured **Jerusalem**. He made Jerusalem the capital of Israel and gave it the names of **Zion** and **City of David.** ("David and all Israel went to Jerusalem...and David took the stronghold of Zion, that is, the City of David.")

1 Chronicles 15: 1-16. David brought the Ark of the Covenant (God's Dwelling Place) to Jerusalem and it became known as the Holy City,

2 Chronicles 28: 2-56. David desired to build a temple but God willed Solomon his son to build it in Jerusalem.

1 Kings 12: 6-33. In 930 BC, Israel was divided into two kingdoms (Israel—the Northern Kingdom and Judah—the Southern Kingdom). **Jerusalem** became the capital of Judah and was plundered several times by various kings.

2 Kings 25: 1-17. After three invasions, beginning in 605 BC, King Nebuchadnezzar captured **Jerusalem** in 586 BC, deported the inhabitants, and destroyed it, leaving only a few peasants.

Ezra 1: 1-3. After 70 years in captivity (using the Jewish calendar for numbering), King Cyrus in 538 BC allowed the Jews under Zerubbabel to return to their homeland of Jerusalem (a Jewish state under the Persian government) to rebuild their Temple. The prophets Zechariah and Haggi urged them on.

Esther 1-10. In 479 - 474 BC, Queen **Esther in Persia** was used by God to save the Jews and all of **Jerusalem** from annihilation.

Ezra 7: 1-10. In 458 BC, Ezra returned to **Jerusalem** to revive the faith of the people and stir a heartfelt commitment to study, obey the law of the Lord and refurbish the temple.

Nehemiah 2. In 444 BC after four months of fasting and prayer, Nehemiah returned to Jerusalem to rebuild the broken city, which he found in terrible ruins with burned down gates, broken walls and broken people.

Timeline for Israel and Judah: Captivities and Returns

	Captivities			*Returns*		
Israel: Ten Northern Tribes	Assyrian Captivity		Jerusalem	Esther saves nation	Jerusalem	Jerusalem
Divided Israel			Return w/ Zerubbabel		Return w/ Ezra	Return w/ Nehemiah
Judah: Two Southern Tribes		Babylonian Captivity	To Rebuild Temple		To Rebuild Faith	To Repair City Walls; to Rebuild Gates and Faith
Scripture	2 Kings 17	Daniel 1 2 Kings 24	Ezra 1-6	Esther	Ezra 7-10	Nehemiah 1-13
930 BC	722 BC	605, 597, 587 BC	536 BC	478 BC	458 BC	445 - 425 BC

Jerusalem in Ruins

The City of Jerusalem and the nation of Judah had been in ruins with burned down gates and broken walls more than once since 605 BC. God had warned Judah (i.e., what was left of Israel) for many years to stop worshipping idols and sacrificing to other gods and practicing immorality, but they would not listen. Starting in 605 BC and continuing until 586 BC, God allowed the Chaldeans under King Nebuchadnezzar to destroy Jerusalem, as well as the Temple and all of Judah. His armies took the young (e.g., Daniel in 605 BC—see Daniel 1) and the old (e.g., the prophet Ezekiel in 586 BC plus the king with his family, the officials, the priests and the warriors—see 2 Kings 24) captive to Babylon, and left only the poor and destitute in the land.

In 538 BC, after the time of 70 years of exile (using Jewish calendar numbering) called the *Babylonian Captivity,* King Cyrus permitted the Jews, led by Zerubbabel, to return to Jerusalem to rebuild their Temple on the site where King Solomon constructed the First Temple. The building process was stopped often because of persecution and opposition, but the temple was finally completed in 515 BC. Then in 458 BC, King Artaxerxes allowed Ezra to return to Jerusalem to refurbish the temple and make offerings, but the city still had ruins, and the people were frustrated by obstruction from their enemies. False rumors spread by those who wanted to profit from the territory and soon caused the king to halt any further repair or refurbishing efforts.

Jerusalem was a holy city to the Jewish nation. It was the capital of Judah and Israel. But it was much more. Jerusalem was a part of Jewish identity. It was intertwined with religion and worship—God's presence was in the temple. To Nehemiah, it was a great shame that the city was broken down and the people were devastated. Without walls and gates and protection, there could be no safety from invaders; there could be no peace, no security, no strength, no city and no nation.

7. ***NEHEMIAH APPROACHES GOD.*** What does v. 5 tell you about the way Nehemiah approached God in prayer?

❖**Ponderings**

a. In v. 5, Nehemiah approached God in prayer by using various names and characteristics of God. Record these names in the following spaces and underline what you learn about the names.

"O ____________________." In Hebrew, the word is "Yahweh" and is the divine personal name that God gave in love and relationship to be used by the people of Israel. [x]

"____________________ of heaven." In Hebrew, the name is "Elohim/ Elohai" and refers to God, the creator of the heavens and earth and the judge of the universe, who reigns throughout all eternity and is unlimited in strength and time. [xi]

"Great and ____________________ God." In Hebrew, the word is "Hael" which means *awesome* and refers to the awe and holy reverence for God expressed in adoration, worship and holy living.[xii] For an example of "Hael" used in Scripture, see *Psalm 66: 3.* "Say to God, "How awesome are your deeds! Because of your power, your enemies cringe before you. All the earth worships you; they sing praises to you, sing praises to your name."

"God who keeps covenant and ____________. In Hebrew, the word is "Chesedh" and it refers to God *who guards His covenant relationship* by keeping His promises of steadfast love and devotion to His people never changed.[xiii] For examples of the use of "Chesedh," see Psalm 40: 11 and 119: 76-77.

Psalm 40: 11. Your steadfast love and your faithfulness keep me safe forever!

Psalm 119: 76-77. Let your steadfast love become my comfort according to your promise to your servant.

b. Which of the names Nehemiah used in approaching God is most meaningful to you? Why?

8. ***NEHEMIAH'S PRAYER.*** According to v. 6, what type prayer would you say Nehemiah's prayer is?

Note. *The Catechism of the Catholic Church* summarizes the basic types of prayer in #2644: "The Holy Spirit is the one who teaches the Church and recalls to her all that Jesus instructs in the life of prayer, inspiring new expressions of the same basic forms of prayer: blessing, petition, intercession, thanksgiving, and praise."

9. ***THEMES OF THE INTERCESSORY PRAYER.*** Nehemiah uses four themes in his prayer. Please list these four themes on the lines below.

   a. ______________________________ (v. 5)

   b. ______________________________ (v. 6-7)

   c. ______________________________ (v. 8-9)

   d. ______________________________ (v.10-11)

Note: *The themes of Nehemiah's prayer* are based on what he would have learned about worship and prayer in His faith and Scripture. (For example, you can read these same themes in David's prayer found in 1 Chronicles 16.)

❖Ponderings

a. Which of the 4 themes do you use in prayer?

b. Which theme do you want to use more in prayer?

Intercessory Prayer - The Four ABCD Themes

Nehemiah was using intercessory prayer for his family and his nation. Intercessory prayer according to the Catechism of the Catholic Church, CCC, #2647, can simply be defined as "asking on behalf of another—it knows no boundaries and even extends to our enemies." The Catholic Encyclopedia further explains intercessory prayer this way, "[T]to intercede is to go or come between two parties, to plead before one of them on behalf of the other."[xiv] Interceding for others in prayer is one of the most loving and power things we can do. James 5: 16 points out its efficacy: "The prayer of the righteous is powerful and effective."

The Bible even describes prayer as a weapon in battle and that we should "Pray in the Spirit at all times in every prayer and supplication and to that end, keep alert and always persevere in supplication for all the saints [i.e., people of God]." In addition, 2 Corinthians 10: 3-5 reminds us that we battle often what we do not see: "Indeed, we live as human beings, but we do not wage war according to human standards; for the weapons of our warfare are not merely human, but they have divine power to destroy strongholds. We destroy arguments and every proud obstacle raised up against the knowledge of God, and we take every thought captive to obey Christ." This kind of heavenly prayer will transform those around us as well as ourselves.

Jesus is the model for powerful intercession. He is the one who pleads on our behalf before the Father. His role is underscored in 1 Timothy 2: 5: "For there is one God; there is also one mediator between God and humankind, Christ Jesus, himself human, who gave himself as ransom for all." As the high priest of our new covenant with God, Hebrews 7:25 tells us: "He [Jesus] is able for all time to save those who approach God through him, since he always lives to make intercession for them." This is something Jesus does all the time for us and will continue to do until we come into eternal life with Him.

The knowledge that Jesus is always interceding for us—for our sins and needs, and that he is always blessing us, uplifts us. It also challenges us to join him in interceding for our nation, our families, ourselves and others. Jesus paid the price for our redemption so we can "confidently approach the throne of grace to receive mercy and to find grace for timely help" (Hebrews 4:16). Jesus desires that we bring all of our concerns, pressures, stresses, problems, needs—big and small —to Him.

As the needs and sufferings in the world increase, we cannot help but want to join Jesus in intercession. Sometimes, we may wonder how to approach intercessory prayer and how to pray effective prayers of intercession. This is where Nehemiah comes in. Starting in Nehemiah 1, he shows us an example of effective intercessory prayer. If we look closely at the themes of Nehemiah's prayer, we can easily remember them. We can use the themes for intercession for our country, our families, our own lives and even for those who do not like us and for whom we do not like!

The ABCDs is an acronym that encompasses the themes of Nehemiah's intercessory prayer that you may find helpful in guiding you in intercessory prayer.

The ABCDs of Intercessory Prayer

- Declare God's awesome greatness— Cry out to the God of all creation, the God of steadfast love for His people, the God of the impossible, the great and righteous Judge of the universe.

- Confess the sins of our nation, our families and ourselves— Nehemiah had a deep love and devotion to God, yet he interceded and confessed the sins of all as if they were all his own.

- Believe the truth of God's Word and His faithfulness – recall and pray aloud Scriptures that show your faith in them.

- Ask God for all those needs that consume your attention, those you see around you—big and small—and use the promises of God's Word. *Supplication* is the term often used in the Bible for humbly asking, even pleading with God in prayer.

Note. Supplication comes from the Latin word "Supplecare," which means "to plead with humility." Its root word is "*supple,*" which involves becoming bendable and adaptable, without stiffness.[xv] Thus, when we supplicate or ask in humility, we will become supple adaptable, and formable in the Lord's hands. He forms us to become more like Him. He forms our prayer. When we worship Him, we become more like Him as 2 Corinthians 3:18 tells us: "All of us, gazing with unveiled face on the glory of the Lord, are being transformed into the same image from glory to glory, as from the Lord who is the Spirit." Jesus molds us and our prayer resembles *Isaiah 64: 8 says, "O Lord, you are our Father; we are the clay, and you are our potter; we are all the work of your hands."*

10. ***PETITIONS***. What two petitions did Nehemiah finally bring to God in v. 11 (i.e., what did he ASK)?

11. ***REFLECTION ON INTERCESSORY PRAYER.*** Please reflect on the principles that caught your attention from this chapter and **record** what principles you will apply to your prayer life. Consider these possibilities:

❖Ponderings

a. **I need to revere God's name and declare God's greatness** in my prayer time. I can start with praise and adoration. (Consider Hebrews 13: 15 - "Through him [Jesus], then, let us continually **offer a sacrifice of praise to God**, that is, the fruit of lips that confess his name," Psalm 100: 4 - "Enter his gates with thanksgiving, and his courts with praise. Give thanks to him, bless his name" and Matthew 6: 9 – [Jesus taught] "Pray then in this way: Our Father in heaven, **hallowed be your name**.")

b. **My prayer should include confession of sin** for myself and nation and family. When I sin against others, I sin against God (Consider Luke 15: 21: [The prodigal son] "Father, I have **sinned against heaven** and before you.")

c. **I should add persistence in my prayer life.** It is important to persevere in prayer and even fast for the most difficult situations as Nehemiah did. (Consider what Jesus taught in Luke 13: 3-7 - "there was a widow who kept coming to him [the judge] and saying, 'Grant me justice against my opponent… he said…because this widow keeps bothering me, I will grant her justice, so that she may not wear me out by **continually coming**.'" [6] And the Lord said, "Listen to what the unjust judge says. [7] And will not God grant justice to his chosen ones who cry to him day and night?")

d. **I should pray with Scriptures in my prayer life.** Praying with Scripture keeps you focused on God and his power with less attention to the desperation of a need. Jesus prayed with Scripture many times—for example, in Matthew 27: 46 and Mark 15:34, He prayed Psalm 22: 1: "My God, my God, why have you forsaken me?" (Consider what Jesus taught in John 15: 7-8 - "If you abide in me, and **my words abide** in you, ask for whatever you wish, and it will be done for you. My Father is glorified by this, that you bear much fruit and become my disciples.")

e. **I should be specific when I ask God for my concerns.** God is interested in the small things as well as the big things in your life so you can feel free to ask him for all your concerns. (Consider Philippians 4: 6-7 - "Do not worry about anything, **but in everything by prayer and supplication** with thanksgiving let your requests be made known to God. And the peace of God, which surpasses all understanding, will guard your hearts and your minds in Christ Jesus.")

Prepare Yourself for Intercessory Prayer – Three Quick Steps

Now is a good time to practice the themes you learned about prayer from Nehemiah. Consider how you can use Nehemiah's example of incorporating the Holy Word of God into your prayer.

A good approach to intercession starts with preparation **by** 1) **writing** down some of your concerns, 2) **listening to God** – invite God to guide you in what He wants you to pray, and 3) **finding/using Scriptures** to praise God's greatness and glory. [xvi]

In summary, keep in mind these suggestions as you prepare for intercessory prayer:

a. **Write.** Pick out one or two concerns— especially personal or family or national or other concerns. (You might refer to question #3, "Ponderings b.") Then write your concerns in the following *personal prayer response #12.*

b. **Listen.** Spend a few minutes in silence and ask God what he wants you to pray about. Try to put aside your own desires or interests that especially occupy your mind. Ask God what's on His heart and mind for you to pray? Listen to what God desires.

c. **Scripture.** Begin your intercessory prayer with Scripture and the ABCD themes demonstrated by Nehemiah. See *Appendix* A for *Declarations and Praises of God's Greatness in Scripture* for verses to help you add Scripture in your intercessions. Write a summary of your prayer in the following *personal prayer response #12.*

12. ***PERSONAL PRAYER RESPONSE TO NEHEMIAH CHAPTER ONE.*** Nehemiah will continue to teach us that no situation or brokenness is beyond God's help and deliverance when we come to Him in intercessory prayer and faith. Nehemiah models how to pray and intercede to our **Awesome** God summarized in the acronym ABCD (starting with D):

- **Declare** God's greatness and faithfulness with praises and Scripture,
- **Confess** our sins and those of our nation and families,
- **Believe** God and His Holy Word, and
- **Ask** for what you need and use Scripture, when possible.

Now, prepare to intercede for yourself, your family and your nation using the ABCD themes.

PREPARE FOR PRAYER

1) Write down the concerns.

MY CONCERNS FOR MY MYSELF, FAMILY AND NATION INCLUDEL:

2) Listen to the Holy Spirit who will guide you in prayer.

3) Recall God's greatness using scripture (see the Appendix for help with *Scriptures for Declaring God's Greatness* and *Praying with Confidence*).

4) Pray and write a summary of your prayer in the space on the next page.

MY INTERCESSORY PRAYER BASED ON NEHEMIAH 1

- **D**eclare God's Greatness (with Scripture)

- **C**onfess the sins of your nation, your family, and yourself with the same passion as if indeed they all belonged to you.

- **B**elieve the truth of God's Word and His Faithfulness by recalling His blessings and the promises in Scripture (use those verses in prayer).

- **A**sk God for the needs He brings to mind. (Let the Holy Spirit lead you in prayer.)

2

GOD IS GRACIOUS!

Connection Question

Can the people closest to you tell when you are sad?

Sorrow of Heart
by Richard Andre
The Coloured Picture Bible for Children, 1875, London
Nehemiah 2: 1, 2

Chapter Two – God is Gracious!

Heartache and Supplication

In our last session, we began reading the Book of Nehemiah, a historical book and the thirteenth book in the Old Testament, taking place around 445 BC.[xvii] We joined Nehemiah as he heard that his beloved homeland and holy city of Jerusalem had been broken down, the gates had been destroyed by fire, and the people were destitute. He wept, fasted, prayed and interceded for four months over the brokenness of the walls, the gates and the people, over 500 miles away. We can relate to Nehemiah's heartache when we consider the brokenness in our nation, our families and our lives. We know those who are broken and need restoration, new strength, healing, revived faith, and hope.

So far Nehemiah has taught us to call out to God in prayer and bring our heartaches to Him in supplication. He has taught us to intercede to our **Awesome** God by **Declaring** His greatness and faithfulness with Praise and Scripture, by **Confessing** our sins and those of our nation and families, by **Believing** God and expressing our belief in His Holy Scripture, and by **Asking**. To *ask* in the Bible can be translated *to supplicate* which means to passionately or intensely pray or even plead your case before God with humility. It comes from the Latin base word "supplecare," which indicates that as we ask in prayer, we will become supple or molded by God to be more like Him in what we ask and who we are.

Today, we will continue to intercede with Nehemiah over the brokenness in our lives, our families, and our nation. We will ask the Lord to take away all fear and put his confidence and his desires into our hearts to begin the rebuilding at all levels.

Chapter Two Questions

1. ***NEHEMIAH 1: 11 AND 2: 1 - 9.*** In preparation for this study, please read Nehemiah 1: 11 and 2: 1-19 *below* and **circle** the verse(s) or ideas that catch your attention. Share or record why these verses caught your attention.

Nehemiah 1: 11

O Lord, let your ear be attentive to the prayer of your servant, and to the prayer of your servants who delight in revering your name. Give success to your servant today, and grant him mercy in the sight of this man." At the time, I was cupbearer to the king.

Nehemiah 2: 1 - 9

In the month of Nisan*, in the twentieth year of King Artaxerxes, when wine was
served him, I carried the wine and gave it to the king. Now, I had never been sad in
his presence before. 2 So the king said to me, "Why is your face sad, since you are not
sick? This can only be sadness of the heart." Then I was very much afraid. 3 I said to
the king, "May the king live forever! Why should my face not be sad, when the city,
the place of my ancestors' graves, lies waste, and its gates have been destroyed by
fire?" 4 Then the king said to me, "What do you request?" So I prayed to the God of
heaven. 5 Then I said to the king, "If it pleases the king, and if your servant has found
favor with you, I ask that you send me to Judah, to the city of my ancestors' graves, so
that I may rebuild it." 6 The king said to me (the queen also was sitting beside him),
"How long will you be gone, and when will you return?" So it pleased the king to
send me, and I set him a date. 7 Then I said to the king, "If it pleases the king, let letters
be given me to the governors of the province Beyond the River, that they may grant
me passage until I arrive in Judah; 8 and a letter to Asaph, the keeper of the king's
forest, directing him to give me timber to make beams for the gates of the temple
fortress, and for the wall of the city, and for the house that I shall occupy."

And the king granted me what I asked, for the gracious hand of my God was upon
me. *9 Then I came to the governors of the province Beyond the River, and gave them
the king's letters. Now the king had sent officers of the army and cavalry with me.

Notes (v. 2:1). *Nisan* (v. 1) on the Hebrew calendar is March-April in 444 BC. *Gracious hand* (v. 8) is often translated "good favor" as in the New American Bible Revised Edition (NABRE), which is the Mass and lectionary translation. *God's gracious hand* in Old Testament Hebrew is an idiom for someone finding "favor with God."

2. ***FOUR MONTHS LATER (V. 1).*** What do you think Nehemiah was doing in the four months that passed between Chapter 1 to Chapter 2 (it was the month of Chislev in Chapter 1 and now it is Nisan)?

❖Ponderings

a. How could the prophet Habakkuk's thoughts after prayer further explain what Nehemiah was doing for four months? Read Habakkuk 2: 1 below.

Habakkuk 2: 1. I will stand at my watch post, and station myself on the rampart; I will keep watch to see what he [God] will say to me, and what he will answer…

b. How could Psalm 95: 6-8 further describe what Nehemiah was doing in intercessory prayer?

Psalm 95: 6-8. O come, let us worship and bow down, let us kneel before the Lord, our Maker! [7] For he is our God, and we are the people of his pasture, and the sheep of his hand...[8] Do not harden your hearts.

3. ***VERY MUCH AFRAID*** (v. 2). What does King Artaxerxes notice about Nehemiah and what does he ask?

❖Ponderings

a. Why do you think Nehemiah was *VERY MUCH AFRAID* (v. 2)?

b. Do you think Nehemiah planned to ask the King for help on that day (refer to Nehemiah 1: 11)? Why or why not?

c. Considering what you read in the following section from Ezra 4, what did Nehemiah know about the King's attitude, twenty years prior, toward the rebuilding of Jerusalem?

Ezra 4: 11 -13, 17, 21. "To King Artaxerxes: Your servants, the people of the province Beyond the River, send greeting. And now [12] may it be known to the king that the Jews who came up from you to us have gone to Jerusalem. They are rebuilding that rebellious and wicked city; they are finishing the walls and repairing the foundations. [13] Now may it be known to the king that, if this city is rebuilt and the walls finished, they will not pay tribute, custom, or toll, and the royal revenue will be reduced...[17] The king [Artaxerxes] sent an answer: ... **[21] Therefore issue an order that these people be made to cease, and that this city not be rebuilt, until I make a decree."**

4. ***NEHEMIAH'S RESPONSE*** (1: 3-5). How does Nehemiah respond to the king questions (v. 3)?

❖Ponderings

a. What does Nehemiah's response show to the king?

b. When the King asked for an answer, what kind of prayer did Nehemiah use immediately (v. 4)?

5. ***THE REQUESTS*** (v. 4-8). In the space below, list the two questions the king asked Nehemiah and Nehemiah's response to each question.

The Kings Question #1 (v. 4-5)	Nehemiah's Response
The Kings Question #2 (v. 6-8)	Nehemiah's Response

❖Ponderings

a. How do Nehemiah's answers show his trust in God?

b. How do Nehemiah's answers demonstrate his discernment and wisdom from God?

6. ***ANSWERED PRAYER*** (v. 8-9). How is the King's response to Nehemiah a sign of "God's gracious hand was upon him" (*God's favor was upon him*)?

❖Ponderings

a. Why would the king be so gracious to Nehemiah to the point of even sending his own officers and army with him (v. 9)?

b. What do Psalm 84: 11-12 and 2 Chronicles 16:9 add to the meaning of *God's gracious hand* or *God's favor*?

Psalm 84: 11-12. For the Lord God is a sun and shield; he **bestows favor** and honor. No good thing does the Lord withhold from those who walk uprightly. 12 O Lord of hosts, happy is everyone who trusts in you.

2 Chronicles 16: 9. For the eyes of the Lord range throughout the entire earth, to strengthen those whose heart is true to him.

7. ***PRAYERFUL PERSISTANCE*** (v. 8-9). What purpose did prayerful persistence, waiting and discernment have during the four months Nehemiah prayed and fasted?

❖Ponderings

a. Read Isaiah 64:4 and Psalm 27: 13-14 *below* and then summarize what these verses teach about the meaning of prayerful persistence.

Isaiah 64: 4. From ages past no one has heard, no ear has perceived, no eye has seen any God besides you, who works for those who **wait** for him.

Psalm 27: 13-14. I believe that I shall see the goodness of the Lord in the land of the living. 14 **Wait for the Lord**; be strong, and let your heart **take courage**; wait for the Lord!

b. How hard is it to wait for an answer from God? What are the benefits of waiting?

The Lord is Gracious, He Gives Favor to Nehemiah

At the conclusion of Nehemiah 1, we read two important details that impact our understanding of Chapter 2. Nehemiah told us, "At the time, I was cupbearer to the king." Earlier we learned that this meant Nehemiah held a high-ranking position with esteem and influence because it was close to the king. He knew the king personally and the king depended on him for his safety and his very life. Nehemiah also told us his most important prayer request: "Give success to your servant today, and grant him mercy in the sight of this man!" *This man* was obviously the KING.

Today we see the fruitfulness of Nehemiah's four months of prayer and fasting and waiting. He prayed for favor with the king and God answered his prayer when one day, the king asked his cupbearer why he looked so sad. Nehemiah had been heartsick for months but it was forbidden for anyone to enter the king's presence showing any dissatisfaction near the king (Esther 4:2). The cupbearer especially could show no negative emotions to the king. On one particular day, Nehemiah's sadness oozed out. He could hold it back no longer and he discerned it was time to move forward. He was prepared for this day with all of his intercession and calling out to God.

Nehemiah remembered that years earlier the king had stopped the rebuilding of Jerusalem because of political accusations against the Jews in Jerusalem. To avoid the king's political sensitivities, Nehemiah refrained from mentioning Jerusalem. Instead, he appealed to a common respect for proper ancestral burial grounds and broken city gates. The king was sympathetic, because the *King of Kings* had opened his heart and given Nehemiah favor. So, the King of Persia, Artaxerxes I granted Nehemiah's request to return to Judea and rebuild the brokenness. In addition, he agreed to send letters with him to the governors for safe travels and to the keeper of the king's forest for acquiring timber for the temple, the city and Nehemiah's own house. The king even sent his army officers and horsemen to accompany him. Wow!! What grace! What favor! The prayer, the fasting, the discernment and the waiting had most certainly paved the way for God to act on the king's heart and lead the way.

8. ***APPLICATION.*** When Nehemiah came to rebuild the physical walls and gates, he would also be rebuilding spiritual brokenness. As you study Nehemiah, please ask God what are the broken areas in your life, spiritual or otherwise (and in your family and in our nation, etc.) that need healing and rebuilding. Then consider what you have learned so far from Nehemiah that can help you begin the refurbishing work:

    a. Write down all the open gates (where you might let darkness or evil into your life such as, sinful habits, addictions to alcohol, drugs, or cigarettes, uncontrolled imaginations, extreme fears, emotional hurts, unforgiveness, filthy television, internet or movies, unrestrained tongue, and family or generational sins) and broken walls (where you need increased strength, fortitude, faith, healing, persistence, prayer) in your life that need restoration. Ask God to show you where the open gates and broken walls are in your life.

    b. Write down any areas where you need to repent and confess sins. Repentance involves a turn-round in direction. Consider where God wants to strengthen you and help you change attitudes of hopelessness, discouragement or procrastination, etc. Ask God and write down what action you will take to confess, repent and turn from sin.

    c. Recall the ***favor*** and ***blessings*** that came to Nehemiah when he confessed, repented, praised God and acted. Write your response to the following questions.

        i. Have you ever prayed for God to **open a door** and make a way before you? ASK HIM FOR AN OPEN DOOR NOW. (You can use the ABCDs of intercession.)

        ii. Have you ever asked God to give you **favor** [put his gracious hand upon you] as Nehemiah did? PRAY FOR HIS FAVOR NOW.

        iii. Have you ever asked God to put **His desires in your heart**, especially on how you can serve HIM by rebuilding your life, your family or your nation? Ask HIM NOW.

iv. Have you asked God **for wisdom** to help with the work of restoring the physical or spiritual brokenness in your life or in others? ASK HIM NOW.

v. Have you *waited* and **persisted in praying** for an answer knowing that change and answers take time? ASK GOD NOW TO HELP YOU PERSIST IN PRAYER (ABCDs) AND REBUILD NOW. Then make it your goal to persist in PRAYER and WAIT prayerfully.

d. How do these verses form Psalm 40 and Proverbs 16 give you courage to ***wait***? Who will be your help as you wait?

Psalm 40: 1-4. I **waited patiently** for the Lord; he inclined to me and heard my
cry. [2] He drew me up from the desolate pit, out of the miry bog, and set my feet
upon a rock, making my steps secure. [3] He put a new song in my mouth, a song
of praise to our God. Many will see and fear, and put their trust in the Lord. [4]
Happy are those who make the Lord their trust … NRSVCE

Proverbs 16: 7. When the ways of people please the Lord, he causes even their enemies to be at peace with them. NRSVCE

9. ***REFLECTIONS ON NEHEMIAH 2.*** Please reflect on the principles that caught your attention from this chapter. Circle and then record in the space that follows which principles you can apply to your life starting today and why.

   a. **Ask God for discernment, instead of worrying.** Nehemiah prayed and fasted for four months before God gave him the discernment and the direction to go ahead. (Isaiah 40:31, "Those who wait for the Lord shall renew their strength, they shall mount up with wings like eagles, they shall run and not be weary, they shall walk and not faint.)

   b. **Wait! Don't give up, God hears and answers prayer.** No situation or brokenness is beyond God's help when we pray. (Also see, Isaiah 59:1, "See, the Lord's hand is not too short to save, nor his ear too dull to hear." Psalm 34: 17, "When the righteous cry for help, the Lord hears, and rescues them from all their troubles. ")

   c. **Respect those in authority.** Honor those in leadership and pray for them, just as Nehemiah spoke the respectful greeting, "May the king live forever." (Also see Romans 13:1, "Let every person be subject to the governing authorities" and 1 Timothy 2:1, "First of all, then, I urge that supplications, prayers, intercessions, and thanksgivings be made for everyone, [2] for kings and all who are in high positions, so that we may lead a quiet and peaceable life in all godliness and dignity.")

   d. **Pray always and often.** Consider using short aspirations or arrow prayers—which are short prayers that can be repeated often throughout your day as Nehemiah, prayed before answering the King (2: 4)," So I prayed to the God of heaven." (Also see 1 Thessalonians 5: 16-18, "Rejoice always, pray without ceasing, give thanks in all circumstances; for this is the will of God in Christ Jesus for you.") For example, you might pray: "Lord Jesus Christ, give me your wisdom."

e. **Call on the Holy Name of Jesus.** The Catechism of the Catholic Church #2668 says, "The invocation of the **holy name of Jesus** is the simplest way of praying always.... This prayer is possible 'at all times' because it is not one occupation among others but the only occupation - that of loving God, which animates and transfigures every action in Christ Jesus." For example, you might pray: "Blessed be the most Holy Name of Jesus without end! Help me now."

f. **Profess your faith in Christ often.** The New Testament mentions the most basic Christian creed can be summarized in three words - "Jesus is Lord" (1 Corinthians 12: 3) or in four words - "Jesus Christ is Lord" (Philippians 2: 11). Uttering the name "Lord" (Kyrios) is also the most distinctively Christian creed because Christ's divinity and lordship over one's life is the distinctive, essential faith of Christians.[xviii]

g. **Be courageous even when fearful.** When you find yourself "very much afraid," pray and stand strong. (See also Joshua 1: 9, "Be strong and courageous; do not be frightened or dismayed, for the Lord your God is with you wherever you go" and Psalm 27: 3, 14, "Though an army encamp against me, my heart shall not fear; though war rise up against me, yet I will be confident…"Wait for the Lord; be strong, and let your heart take courage; wait for the Lord!")

10. ***PERSONAL PRAYER RESPONSE.*** In this chapter Nehemiah has taught us that no brokenness is beyond God's hand of deliverance when we come to Him in prayer and faith. God wants to lead us. Nehemiah models how to pray and intercede to our **Awesome** God summarized in the acronym ABCD (starting with D):

   a. **Declare** God's greatness and faithfulness with praises and Scripture,

   b. **Confess** our sins and those of our nation and families,

   c. **Believe** God and His Holy Word, and

   d. **Ask** for what you need and use Scripture, when possible.

Now, prepare to intercede for yourself, your family and your nation using the ABCD themes.

PREPARE FOR PRAYER

1) Write down your concerns.

MY CONCERNS FOR MYSELF, FAMILY NATION INCLUDE:

2) Listen to the Holy Spirit who will guide you in prayer.

3) Recall God's greatness using scripture (see the Appendix for help with *Scriptures for Declaring God's Greatness* and *Praying with Confidence*).

4) Pray and write a summary of your prayer in the space on the next page.

INTERCESSORY PRAYER BASED ON NEHEMIAH 1: 11-2: 9

- **D**eclare God's Greatness (with Scripture)

- **C**onfess the sins of your nation, your family, and yourself with the same passion as if indeed they all belonged to you.

- **B**elieve the truth of God's Word and His Faithfulness by recalling His blessings and the promises in Scripture (use those verses in prayer).

- **A**sk God for the needs He brings to mind. (Let the Holy Spirit lead you in prayer.)

3

THE NIGHT RIDER

Connection Question

Do you like to work in teams or do you prefer to do a job on your own?

Nehemiah Surveys the Ruins at Night[xix]
by Charles Horne, 1909
The Bible and its Story
Nehemiah 2:1 1-13

Chapter Three - The Night Rider

Two Months Later

In the last chapter, we joined Nehemiah serving wine to King Artaxerxes when the king asked Nehemiah why his face was so sad. Nehemiah hid his feelings from the king for four months while he wept, fasted, repented and interceded on behalf of the broken city of Jerusalem and its destitute people, including his family. But on this day, he could no longer hold it in, his sadness oozed out plus he discerned it was the time to let the king hear of the problem. He was scared because he knew the king would not like hearing "bad news." Actually, it was forbidden in Persian law for any royal servant to show unhappiness or negative emotion before the king. Doing so could result in expulsion from the court or even execution.[xx]

When the king asked what he requested, Nehemiah was prepared to answer because of his intercessions. He was relying on all the wisdom and discernment God gave him. He knew that years earlier the king had stopped the rebuilding of Jerusalem because of political accusations against the Jews in Jerusalem. To avoid the king's political sensitivities, he told the king about the plight of his people and the city, but he did not use the name Jerusalem. Instead, he appealed to a common respect for proper ancestral burial grounds and broken city gates. The king was sympathetic, because the King of Kings had opened his heart and gave Nehemiah favor with Artaxerxes. So the King of Persia granted Nehemiah's request to return to Judea and rebuild his city. He gave him all that he asked for-- papers, protection and even access to the wood in the king's forest. God put the desire in Nehemiah's heart and then opened the way for him to fulfill His calling to rebuild the Jerusalem and the faith of the people.

Chapter Three Questions

1. ***NEHEMIAH 2: 6 -19.*** In preparation for this study, please read Nehemiah 2: 6-19 *below* and **circle** the obstacles that Nehemiah encountered. Share or record your thoughts on these obstacles after Nehemiah had prayed so much prayer.

Nehemiah 2: 6 - 19

The king said to me (the queen also was sitting beside him), "How long will you be gone,
and when will you return?" So it pleased the king to send me, and I set him a date. 7 Then
I said to the king, "If it pleases the king, let letters be given me to the governors of the
province *Beyond the River*, that they may grant me passage until I arrive in Judah; 8 and a
letter to Asaph, the keeper of the king's forest, directing him to give me timber to make
beams for the gates of the temple fortress, and for the wall of the city, and for the house
that I shall occupy." And the king granted me what I asked, for the gracious hand of my
God was upon me.*

Sent to Judah

9 Then I came to the governors of the province *Beyond the River*, and gave them the king's
letters. Now the king had sent officers of the army and cavalry with me. 10 When Sanballat
the Horonite and Tobiah the Ammonite official heard this, it displeased them greatly that
someone had come to seek the welfare of the people of Israel.

Nehemiah's Inspection of the Walls

11 So I came to Jerusalem and was there for three days*. 12 Then I got up during the night, I
and a few men with me; I told no one what my God had put into my heart to do for
Jerusalem. The only animal I took was the animal I rode. 13 I went out by night by the
Valley Gate past the Dragon's Spring and to the Dung Gate, and I inspected the walls of
Jerusalem that had been broken down and its gates that had been destroyed by fire. 14
Then I went on to the Fountain Gate and to the King's Pool; but there was no place for the
animal I was riding to continue. 15 So I went up by way of the valley by night and
inspected the wall. Then I turned back and entered by the Valley Gate, and so returned. 16
The officials did not know where I had gone or what I was doing; I had not yet told the
Jews, the priests, the nobles, the officials, and the rest that were to do the work.

Decision to Restore the Walls

17 Then I said to them, "You see the trouble we are in, how Jerusalem lies in ruins with its
gates burned. Come, let us rebuild the wall of Jerusalem, so that we may no longer suffer
disgrace." 18 I told them that the hand of my God had been gracious upon me, and also the
words that the king had spoken to me. Then they said, "Let us start building!" So they
committed themselves to the common good. 19 But when Sanballat the Horonite and
Tobiah the Ammonite official, and Geshem the Arab heard of it, they mocked and
ridiculed us, saying, "What is this that you are doing? Are you rebelling against the
king?" 20 Then I replied to them, "The God of heaven is the one who will give us success,
and we his servants are going to start building; but you have no share or claim or historic
right in Jerusalem." NRSVCE

Notes. For Nehemiah 2:8, the New American Bible, Revised Edition (NABRE) translates v. 8 with the word "FAVOR" instead of "the gracious hand of God was upon me," It reads: "Since I enjoyed the good **favor** of my God, the king granted my requests."

The time frame of *Susa to Jerusalem* covers five months**.** The events of v. 10-19 take place about two to five months after those of v. 1-9. This was due to the amount of time it took Nehemiah to make the 500-mile journey from Susa to Jerusalem.

Sanballet and Tobiah were governors. *Sanballat the Horonite* was governor of the province of Samaria and as a Horonite was a native of Horonaim, a city of Moab. A letter from the Jews living at Elephantine in southern Egypt (dated 408–407 B.C.) mentions "Delayah and Shelemyah, the sons of Sanballat, the governor of Samaria," and papyri discovered in the Wadi ed-Dâliyeh in the Jordan Valley refer to a Sanballat, governor of Samaria, during the last years of Persian reign. His name in Babylonian was Sinuballit, or "Sin," meaning, *the moon god has given life. Tobiah the Ammonite* was the governor of the province of Ammon in Transjordan. His title was *officer* or *public servant* (in Hebrew, "*ebed*"), which could also be translated "*slave*." Nehemiah may have used this name because of Tobiah's great opposition to God and his people. The Tobiahs remained a powerful family in Maccabean times.[xxi] Sanballat and Tobiah, together with Geshem the Arab (Nehemiah 2:19; 6:1–2) were probably in charge of Edom and the regions to the south and southeast of Judah.

2. ***LOOMING OBSTACLES (V. 10, 19).*** What obstacles awaited Nehemiah?

❖Ponderings

a. Why do you think "Sanballat the Horonite" (governor of Samaria), and "Tobiah the Ammonite" (governor of Transjordan), who held these positions under Persian rule, reacted the way they did to Nehemiah? Why were they so displeased?

b. Who was really behind Nehemiah's desire to rebuild Jerusalem (v. 12)?

3. ***NIGHT RIDER (1: 11-16).*** Describe Nehemiah's activity in the middle of the night.

❖Ponderings

a. Why do you think Nehemiah was surveying the situation in secret?

b. Why is important to be prayerful and tight-lipped at times before taking on any project?

c. How was Nehemiah fulfilling Luke 14: 28-33?

Luke 14: 28-33. For which of you, intending to build a tower, does not first sit down
and estimate the cost, to see whether he has enough to complete it? [29] Otherwise,
when he has laid a foundation and is not able to finish, all who see it will begin to
ridicule him, [30] saying, 'This fellow began to build and was not able to finish.' [31] Or
what king, going out to wage war against another king, will not sit down first and
consider whether he is able with ten thousand to oppose the one who comes against
him with twenty thousand? [32] If he cannot, then, while the other is still far away, he
sends a delegation and asks for the terms of peace.

God Gives Nehemiah Desire, Discernment and Favor

Nehemiah was a prayerful man—he had a relationship with God. He was also in a position and relationship with the one person who could restart the rebuilding—the King. Nehemiah was prepared with all his prayer and fasting, and his reliance on the wisdom and discernment God had given him. He was in a place of honor at the Kings palace. Before his brethren visited with the bleak report, and before his praying, it likely never entered his mind to help rebuild Jerusalem.

From Nehemiah 2: 12, we learn what we had already surmised; it was God who had put the desire in Nehemiah's heart to rebuild Jerusalem. The more time Nehemiah spent in prayer (four months here), the more God changed his desires and his life. It was God who would give him wisdom and discernment. Spending time with God in prayer is always the way to line up your desires with God's desires for you and to find God's wisdom and guidance. God wants to guide you to the place where you can be most fulfilled and fruitful. He wants to give you His favor. You will never regret asking God for His wisdom, His favor and His direction. Jesus said in John 10: 10, "I came that they may have life, and have it **abundantly."** GOD IS FOR YOU. HE HAS YOUR BEST IN MIND.

Nehemiah immediately used Godly wisdom and discernment via night riding and his investigation of Jerusalem. The city was in ruins and he did not want anyone to oppose the work before it could get started. The enemies of the faith and rebuilding efforts soon appeared on the scene. Sanballat and Tobiah were leaders in the surrounding provinces of Samaria and Ammon; Geshem was a leader in Arab territory. To them, a restored Jewish province would be a threat to their trade and authority. Actually, they had many reasons to oppose the rebuilding, including: 1) they already had bad generational tensions from the time when Zerubbabel refused the Samaritan's help (e.g., Ezra 4: 1-6), 2) the rebuilding threatened their positions of leadership because Nehemiah had the King's appointment for leading the reconstruction, 3) the increased number of returnees endangered their control as the numbers could eventually arise against their authority, and finally, 4) Sanballat, Tobiah, and Geshem who were engaged in corrupt and crooked money-making projects, feared their lucrative efforts might be exposed or shut down.

4. ***ENCOURAGING WORDS.*** What kind of encouragement does Nehemiah offer his people (v. 17-18)?

❖Ponderings

a. How did Nehemiah motivate them to rebuild (v. 18)?

b. When they were disgraced, discouraged, and reticent to rebuild, how did Nehemiah challenge them to move beyond past sufferings, hardships and challenges?

c. How did Nehemiah offer hope to the people with his testimony of God's guidance?

d. Although we are not rebuilding our city, we are rebuilding the Kingdom of God—in people's hearts and minds. How are you discouraged in rebuilding the spiritual gates in your family, friends or nation?

e. What difference does it make to know that God is with you in the rebuilding? What hope does it give you? Remind yourself of how God has helped you in the past.

5. ***THE OBSTACLES.*** What obstacles did the enemies throw at Nehemiah and his people (v. 19)?

6. ***DECLARING GOD'S PRESENCE IN OBSTACLES.*** How did Nehemiah respond to the derision from his enemies (v. 20)?

❖Ponderings

a. How can you declare God's presence and guidance in what you are doing?

b. How could it make a difference in what you are facing?

7. ***CHALLENGES.*** Nehemiah knew there would be some challenges in rebuilding Jerusalem. What gave him hope and kept him from becoming discouraged or giving up?

❖Ponderings

a. Did God know there would be a lot of challenges in rebuilding Jerusalem?

b. Why didn't God remove all the challenges and enemies that Nehemiah would face?

c. When you encounter challenges, does that mean that God is NOT motivating you to do the work He puts in your life?

d. Where can you go to find hope for your rebuilding efforts?

8. ***REFLECTION ON THE CHAPTER.*** Please reflect on the principles that caught your attention from this chapter. Circle the ones that apply most to you and record the principles you can apply to your life starting today and why.

a. **Ask God to put His desires on your heart.** God has deep desires for each of us. Maybe you have never asked God what His deepest desire for you is. Maybe you have never asked Him to give you His desires for your life. Now would be a good time to ask God to put His desires in your heart. God will never disappoint you. He always wants to bring you to your best self and fulfillment. (Also see Psalm 37: 4. "Take delight in the Lord, and he will give you the desires of your heart.")

b. **Ask God for *favor* this week.** God gave Nehemiah favor with the king and the king gave him more than he could imagine. Please consider where you need ***favor*** when approaching a person or a challenge. Then ask God for *favor* meaning that the *good hand of God be upon you* (Nehemiah 2: 8) as you approach problems and rebuild faith or brokenness this week? (Also see Genesis 39:21, "But the LORD was with Joseph and extended kindness to him, and gave him *favor* in the sight of the chief jailer" and Psalm 84:11 "For the Lord God is a sun and shield; the Lord bestows *favor* and honor. No good thing does he withhold from those who walk uprightly.")

c. **Give hope to others this week.** Nehemiah shared his testimony of how God was with Him, helped Him and called him to this work. Please consider where you can offer hope to others this week and where you can share your testimony of how God has helped you. Ask God to bring to you those who need to hear the message of hope. (Also see Jeremiah 29:11, "For I know the thoughts that I think toward you, says the LORD, thoughts of peace and not of evil, to give you a future and a hope," Romans 15:4, "For whatever was written in former days was written for our instruction, that through endurance and through the encouragement of the Scriptures we might have hope," and "Romans 15:13, May the God of hope fill you with all joy and peace in believing, so that by the power of the Holy Spirit you may abound in hope.")

d. **Surrender your problems to God and abandon yourself to Him.** Don't give up when you face challenges or opposition. Instead, trust God to lead you. Nehemiah surrendered his problems to the Great and Awesome God in Heaven with passionate prayer and a heart of total abandonment, trusting in his Father's providential care for him. In the same way, you can abandon yourself to our heavenly Father and pray with St. Charles Foucault's *Prayer of Abandonment*:

PRAYER OF ABANDONMENT
by St. Charles de Foucauld (1858-1916)

Father, I abandon myself into your hands;
Do with me what you will.
Whatever you may do, I thank you;
I am ready for all, I accept all.

Let only your will be done in me,
and in all your creatures -
I wish no more than this, O Lord.

Into Your hands I commend my soul;
I offer it to you with all the love of my heart,
for I love you Lord and so need to give myself,
to surrender myself into Your hands
without reserve,
and with boundless confidence,
for You are my Father.

9. ***ACTIONS.*** Nehemiah prayed, rested, listened and explored before he began the rebuilding project. Where do you need to pray, rest, listen, and explore before you dive into a project, especially where there has been a past problem?

    a. Read the following verses and describe what they add to the importance of resting, praying and listening to God before rebuilding.

       Proverbs 24:3. By wisdom a house is built, and by understanding it is established.

       Ephesians 5: 15-16. Look carefully then how you walk, not as unwise but as wise, making the best use of the time, because the days are evil. Therefore, do not be foolish, but understand what the will of the Lord is.

    b. Read the following verses about building, resting and praying. Then record how they inspire you to start praying, reading Scripture, drawing close to Jesus, and resting in Him today before you start rebuilding.

Matthew 7: 24-27. "Everyone then who hears these **words** of mine and **acts** on them will be like a wise man who built his house on rock. [25] The rain fell, the floods came, and the winds blew and beat on that house, but it did not fall, because it had been founded on rock. [26] And everyone who hears these words of mine and does not act on them will be like a foolish man who built his house on sand. [27] The rain fell, and the floods came, and the winds blew and beat against that house, and it fell—and great was its fall!"

Psalm 127: 1. "Unless the Lord builds the house, those who build it labor in vain. Unless the Lord guards the city, the guard keeps watch in vain. [2] It is in vain that you rise up early and go late to rest, eating the bread of anxious toil; for he gives sleep to his beloved."

10. ***PERSONAL PRAYER RESPONSE.*** Nehemiah has taught us that no brokenness is beyond God's repair and renewal when we come to Him in prayer and faith. God wants to lead you. Nehemiah models how to pray and intercede to our God as summarized in the acronym ABCD (starting with D):

    1) **Declare** God's greatness and faithfulness with praises and Scripture,

    2) **Confess** our sins and those of our nation and families,

    3) **Believe** God and His Holy Word, and

    4) **Ask** for what you need and use Scripture, when possible.

Remember to spend a few minutes in silence asking God what He wants you to pray for yourself, your family or nation. Then plan to pray with a Psalm or other Scripture as part of your intercessions. Use the ABCD themes.

Now, prepare to intercede for yourself, your family and your nation using the ABCD themes.

PREPARE FOR PRAYER

1) Write down your concerns.

MY CONCERNS, OPEN GATES, AND BROKENNESS this week INCLUDE:

2) Listen to the Holy Spirit who will guide you in prayer.

3) Recall God's greatness using scripture (see the Appendix for help with *Scriptures for Declaring God's Greatness* and *Praying with Confidence*).

4) Pray and write a summary of your prayer in the space on the next page.

MY INTERCESSORY PRAYER BASED ON NEHEMIAH 2: 6-20

- **D**eclare God's Greatness (with Scripture)

- **C**onfess the sins of your nation, your family, and yourself with the same passion as if indeed they all belonged to you.

- **B**elieve the truth of God's Word and His Faithfulness by recalling His blessings and the promises in Scripture (use those verses in prayer).

- **A**sk God for the needs He brings to mind. (Let the Holy Spirit lead you in prayer.)

4

MEET THE WORKERS

Connection Question

How do our families, churches, communities and nation need spiritual rebuilding?

The People Rebuilding the Walls of Jerusalem[xxii]
St. Takia.org
Nehemiah 3

Chapter Four - Meet the Workers

Night-time Surveillance

In our last session, we read how God gave Nehemiah favor with Artaxerxes, King of Persia, who granted Nehemiah's request to return to Judah and rebuild his city. He gave him papers, protection and even access to the wood in the king's forest plus he sent along a military guard to keep him safe—this was more than what he requested. Through Nehemiah's intercession, God had put the desire in his heart to fulfill His calling to help rebuild Jerusalem and the faith of His people and the favor to succeed with the task.

Nehemiah first rested and then used Godly wisdom and discernment in a nighttime surveillance of Jerusalem. The city was in ruins and he did not want anyone to oppose the work before it could get started. Nehemiah was able to motivate the people to begin the work by sharing his testimony of how God's gracious hand (good favor) was upon them as the king had provided the many supplies. Although the ruins had accumulated over many years, the people were now inspired and replied, "Let us begin the good work." As expected, the enemies of God appeared. Sanballet, Tobiah, and Geshem saw the rebuilding as a threat to their authority and lucrative moneymaking deals so they quickly appeared on the scene to mock and ridicule the people of God. Nehemiah responded by proclaiming: "The God of heaven is the one who will give us success, and we his servants are going to start building; but you have no share or claim or historic right in Jerusalem."

Chapter Four Questions

1. ***NEHEMIAH 3.*** In preparation for this study, please read Nehemiah 3: 1-32 and **circle** all the names of *gates and towers*. Next underline all *professions* (including priests, rulers, nobles or governors, etc.) and make a square house around every mention of *house or chambers*. Finally, place curly lines (flower-like) around all the words, "next to," "after," and "beside." Share what caught your attention.

Nehemiah 3: 1-32

Then the high priest Elisheba set to work with his fellow priests and rebuilt the *Sheep Gate*. They consecrated it and set up its doors; they consecrated it as far as the *Tower of the Hundred* and as far as the *Tower of Hananel*. 2 And the men of Jericho built next to him. And next to them Zaccur son of Imri built.

3 The sons of Hassenaah built the *Fish Gate*; they laid its beams and set up its doors, its bolts, and its bars. 4 Next to them Meremoth son of Uriah son of Hakkoz made repairs. Next to them Meshullam son of Berechiah son of Meshezabel made repairs. Next to them Zadok son of Baana made repairs. 5 Next to them the Tekoites made repairs; but their nobles would not put their shoulders to the work of their Lord.

6 Joiada son of Paseah and Meshullam son of Besodeiah repaired the *Old Gate;* they laid its beams and set up its doors, its bolts, and its bars. 7 Next to them repairs were made by Melatiah the Gibeonite and Jadon the Meronothite—the men of Gibeon and of Mizpah—who were under the jurisdiction of the governor of the province *Beyond the River*. 8 Next to them Uzziel son of Harhaiah, one of the goldsmiths, made repairs. Next to him Hananiah, one of the perfumers, made repairs; and they restored Jerusalem as far as the *Broad Wall*. 9 Next to them Rephaiah son of Hur, ruler of half the district of Jerusalem, made repairs. 10 Next to them Jedaiah son of Harumaph made repairs opposite his house; and next to him Hattush son of Hashabneiah made repairs. 11 Malchijah son of Harim and Hasshub son of Pahath-moab repaired another section and the *Tower of the Ovens*. 12 Next to him Shallum son of Hallohesh, ruler of half the district of Jerusalem, made repairs, he and his daughters.

13 Hanun and the inhabitants of Zanoah repaired the *Valley Gate;* they rebuilt it and set up its doors, its bolts, and its bars, and repaired a thousand cubits of the wall, as far as the *Dung Gate*.

14 Malchijah son of Rechab, ruler of the district of Bethhaccherem, repaired the *Dung Gate;*
he rebuilt it and set up its doors, its bolts, and its bars.
15 And Shallum son of Col-hozeh, ruler of the district of Mizpah, repaired the *Fountain*
Gate; he rebuilt it and covered it and set up its doors, its bolts, and its bars; and he built
the wall of the *Pool of Shelah* of the king's garden, as far as the stairs that go down from the
City of David.

16 After him Nehemiah son of Azbuk, ruler of half the district of Beth-zur, repaired from a
point opposite the graves of David, as far as the artificial pool and the house of the
warriors. 17 After him the Levites made repairs: Rehum son of Bani; next to him
Hashabiah, ruler of half the district of Keilah, made repairs for his district. 18 After him
their kin made repairs: Binnui, son of Henadad, ruler of half the district of Keilah; 19 next
to him Ezer son of Jeshua, ruler of Mizpah, repaired another section opposite the ascent to
the *armory at the Angle.* 20 After him Baruch son of Zabbai repaired another section from
the *Angle* to the door of the house of the high priest Eliashib. 21 After him Meremoth son of
Uriah son of Hakkoz repaired another section from the door of the house of Eliashib to the
end of the house of Eliashib. 22 After him the priests, the men of the surrounding area,
made repairs. 23 After them Benjamin and Hasshub made repairs opposite their house.
After them Azariah son of Maaseiah son of Ananiah made repairs beside his own house. 24
After him Binnui son of Henadad repaired another section, from the house of Azariah to
the Angle and to the corner. 25 Palal son of Uzai repaired opposite the *Angle* and the tower
projecting from the upper house of the king at the court of the guard. After him Pedaiah
son of Parosh 26 and the temple servants living on *Ophel* made repairs up to a point
opposite the *Water Gate* on the east and the projecting tower. 27 After him the Tekoites
repaired another section opposite the great projecting tower as far as the *wall of Ophel.*

28 Above the *Horse Gate* the priests made repairs, each one opposite his own house. 29 After
them Zadok son of Immer made repairs opposite his own house. After him Shemaiah son
of Shecaniah, the keeper of the *East Gate,* made repairs. 30 After him Hananiah son of
Shelemiah and Hanun sixth son of Zalaph repaired another section. After him Meshullam
son of Berechiah made repairs opposite his living quarters. 31 After him Malchijah, one of
the goldsmiths, made repairs as far as the house of the temple servants and of the
merchants, opposite the *Muster Gate,* and to the upper room of the corner. 32 And between
the upper room of the corner and the *Sheep Gate* the goldsmiths and the merchants made
repairs.

2. ***THE GATES***. How many gates were there?

❖Ponderings

a. Why is rebuilding the gates so important to the people?

b. Why do you think it took Nehemiah coming to town to get the rebuilding of the gates started?

c. Do you see any meaning to Jerusalem in the names for each of the gates? What comes to mind?

The Gates

In ancient cities, like Jerusalem, the gates were very important to the people and their existence. Gates were entrances to the city. They provided military protection. The walls of a city represented strength and the gates had chambers with four sets of doors where there were spaces for defence between each door. [xxiii]

Right outside the gates, there were often stalls for traders or anyone who wanted to sell their goods (i.e., mini-malls or farmer's markets in today's vernacular). Right inside the gates, there would be meeting places for the leaders and for those seeking justice (e.g., see Proverbs 31: 23). If there were damaged walls and no gates, the loss of protection, commerce, justice and meeting spaces would be great.

3. ***REPAIRING AND REBUILDING***. How would you describe the rebuilding efforts of the people and everyone's contribution?

❖Ponderings

a. Why would attention go to rebuilding the Sheep Gate **first** (v. 1-3)?

b. Why would the phrase "sons of" be repeated so often and in each section of Nehemiah 3, starting with v. 3?

c. Why do you think all workers' names and their work were recorded here?

4. ***THE OCCUPATIONS OF THE BUILDERS***. List 1) the occupations of the following people who were involved in rebuilding and 2) what they repaired.

Name	Occupation	Gate Repaired
• Eliashib (v. 1)		
• Uzziel (v. 8)		
• Hanahiah (v. 8)		
• Rephaiah (v. 9)		
• Shallum (v. 12)		
• Malchijah (v. 14)		
• Shallum (v. 15)		
• Nehemiah, son of Azbuk, (v. 16)		
• The Temple servants (v. 26)		

❖Ponderings

a. Who did not want to help in the rebuilding (v. 5)?

b. Were women involved in the rebuilding process (v. 12)?

5. ***THE TEN GATES***. Read the following list and descriptions for the ten gates of Jerusalem. Then circle the ones you find most interesting or symbolic for you.

The Ten Gates

In Jerusalem, at the time of Nehemiah, there were 10 gates to the city. In Hebrew, each of the gates had a significant name, which related to its use.

1. **The *Sheep Gate*** was where the sheep were herded into the city to be used as alter sacrifices in the temple. As outlined in Leviticus 1: 3-7 and 6: 8-13, sacrificial lambs were slaughtered and the blood was drained and splashed on the sides of the altar. Then the carcass was given to the presiding priest who laid it upon the fires of the altar to become a pure gift to the Lord as atonement for sin.[xxiv] (Obviously, we can find the symbolism in this gate for us. It can represent Jesus Christ and His Passion, death and resurrection for our sins. He is our gate to eternal life. (For example, see John 10: 8-10: "Very truly, I [Jesus Christ] tell you, I am the **gate for the sheep**. All who came before me are thieves and bandits; but the sheep did not listen to them. **I am the gate.** Whoever enters by me will be saved, and will come in and go out and find pasture. The thief comes only to steal and kill and destroy. I came that they may have life, and have it abundantly."

2. **The *Fish Gate*** was where fish were brought into the city from the Jordan River and the Mediterranean Sea. A fish market was likely nearby where people could buy fish for their homes in the city. (As Christian, fish is always symbolism for us. We can't help but remember Jesus' call to his disciples to become fishers of men and women. For example, see Matthew 4:18, where Jesus "walked by the Sea of Galilee" and "saw two brothers, Simon, who is called Peter, and Andrew his brother, casting a net into the sea—for they were fishermen. And he said to them, 'Follow me, and I will make you fish for people.'")

3. **The *Old Gate*** (also called the Yeshanah Gate) was one of the very first gates in Jerusalem and probably the oldest. (The Old Gate might symbolize for us the great foundation of our faith laid many centuries ago. It is old and we rejoice in its foundation. At a time when it seems like everything is changing, we have this sure hope of Malachi 3:6 says: "For I, the Lord, do not change" and of Hebrews 13: 8: "Jesus Christ is the same yesterday and today and forever.")

4. **The *Valley Gate*** led from a valley into the city of Jerusalem. It must have been very joyful and comforting for travelers when they walked up from the valley into the city, they called home. (The valley gate could symbolize for us the times we felt in a valley, overwhelmed by sin or darkness and Jesus comes to comfort us. In John 10: 9, Jesus says: "I am the gate. Whoever enters by me will be saved, and will come in and go out and find pasture" and 2 Corinthians 1: 3-4 reminds us: "Blessed be the God and Father of our Lord Jesus Christ, the Father of mercies and the God of all consolation, who consoles us in all our affliction, so that we may be able to console those who are in any affliction with the consolation with which we ourselves are consoled by God.")

5. **The *Dung Gate*** was the place where the garbage and manure were carried out of the city of Jerusalem. If garbage built up in a city, the whole city was in trouble—a huge stink would smell everywhere and the people's health would be threatened. So, the Dung Gate was essential for getting rid of all garbage. (Fortunately for us, Jesus is the one carries out the sin garbage from our lives through confession, repentance and receiving his forgiveness. We are reminded of this in 1 John 1: 7-10: "If we walk in the light as he himself is in the light, we have fellowship with one another, and the blood of Jesus his Son cleanses us from all sin. If we say that we have no sin, we deceive ourselves, and the truth is not in us. If we confess our sins, he who is faithful and just will forgive us our sins and cleanse us from all unrighteousness.")

6. **The *Fountain Gate*** was located hear the pool of Siloam and was the place where the people would get water for cleansing themselves before going into the temple. The Siloam Pool likely refers to the place where King Hezekiah diverted some of the water from his Siloam tunnel (see 2 Kings 20: 20) to provide water for the royal gardens and for those travelers, who would come for it. (For us the symbolism of a fountain is beautiful. Jesus is the *Fountain of Eternal Life.* In John 4: 13, he told the woman at the well "Everyone who drinks of this water will be thirsty again, but those who drink of the water that I will give them will never be thirsty. The water that I will give will become in them a spring of water gushing up to eternal life.")

7. **The *Water Gate*** was the gate where water was brought into Jerusalem. It was near a spring-fed waterway that led into the city. It didn't seem to need repair as the work was done around it, but none was noted as done to it (Nehemiah 3: 36). This is the gate where Ezra will later stand and read the Word of God to the people (Nehemiah 8: 1-4). (For us today, Psalm 42: 1 reminds us of our thirst, "As a deer longs for flowing streams, so my soul longs for you, O God." We long for intimacy with God, for the life-giving Eucharist and for the Word of God. Basil the Great, Bishop of Caesarea, Doctor of the Church, and Defender of the Christian faith in the fourth century spoke about the importance of reading and praying the Scriptures daily.[xxv] He called the Holy Scriptures a "pharmacy" of medicine matched to our own illnesses and the Psalms a "jewel case of remedies for all of our cases.")

8. **The *Horse Gate,*** located next to the horse stables, was the place where the riders on horses would depart. Often, they would ride out from this gate into battle to defend the city from attacks. (Today, the horse gate might remind us of the battle of spiritual warfare. We face it every day, whether we realize it or not. Pope Francis says,

> "We are all tempted because the law of our spiritual life, our Christian life is a struggle. That's because the Prince of this world, Satan, doesn't want our holiness, he doesn't want us to follow Christ. Maybe some of you might say: 'But Father, how old-fashioned you are to speak about the devil in the 21st century!' But look out because the devil is present! The devil is here . . . even in the 21st century! And we must not be naïve, right? We must learn from the Gospel how to fight against Satan." [xxvi]

Ephesians 6: 10-18 tells us what to do: "Finally, be strong in the Lord and in the strength of his power. Put on the whole armor of God, so that you may be able to stand against the wiles of the devil. For our struggle is not against enemies of blood and flesh, but against the rulers, against the authorities, against the cosmic powers of this present darkness, against the spiritual forces of evil in the heavenly places. Therefore, take up the whole armor of God, so that you may be able to withstand on that evil day, and having done everything, to stand firm. Stand therefore, and fasten the belt of truth around your waist, and put on the breastplate of righteousness. As shoes for your feet put on whatever will make you ready to proclaim the gospel of peace. With all of these, take the shield of faith, with which you will be able to quench all the flaming arrows of the evil one. Take the helmet of salvation, and the sword of the Spirit, which is the word of God. Pray in the Spirit at all times in every prayer and supplication. To that end keep alert and always persevere in supplication for all the saints.")

9. The ***East Gate*** faces the Mount of Olives and the rising sun so it was the first gate opened each morning. (Today, this gate might symbolize the importance of Morning Prayer or meeting the Lord at the start of every day with prayer and thanksgiving. Psalm 130: 5-6 reminds us: "I wait for the Lord, my soul waits, and in his word, I hope; my soul waits for the Lord more than those who watch for the morning.")

10. **The *Muster or Inspection Gate*** was the place where at one time David inspected his troops. It was also used as the place where strangers entered the city for the first time. (Today, this gate might be a reminder of the importance of daily examining our consciences and then confessing our sins and receiving His forgiveness. Psalm 32: 5 reminds us of this: "Then I acknowledged my sin to you, and I did not hide my iniquity; I said, "I will confess my transgressions to the Lord," and you forgave the guilt of my sin. " Acts 3: 19-20 affirms the refreshment from a clear conscience: "Repent therefore, and turn to God so that your sins may be wiped out, so that times of refreshing may come from the presence of the Lord…")

6. ***THE PEOPLE'S CONTRIBUTION*** (v. 17-32). Based on your curly lines drawn in question #1, what do you learn about the community effort among God's people?

❖Ponderings

a. Where did each one build (v. 28-29)?

b. What comforting application can you make from this example about God as well as your expectations for where you can rebuild faith and hope?

Teamwork: Everyone's Effort Needed

One of the important gleanings of Nehemiah Chapter 3 is how the people from every vocation and walk of life worked together to accomplish what once seemed like a daunting project. It took everyone's efforts and commitment. Each person had something to give to the work. They only had to offer what they could, even if their vocation didn't fit the task. A perfumer and a goldsmith made repairs (v. 8), which were unrelated to their daily and sophisticated work. However, the nobles felt it was beneath them to do hard work with the other men, so they refused (v. 5).

The rebuilding efforts often began next to each person's own house or chamber. They took care of their own areas first so that their homes were strong and could protect the neighboring walls. The principle is clear; we need to take care our own lives, families and communities, as they are the building blocks that will form a strong Christian church, community and nation.

The work was essential but it was a work of service. No one was paid. All the work was done for the glory of God—for the place of worship, for the people of God. When we work for God, seldom do we feel overlooked or unappreciated in the process as God gets the Glory not us. The verses from Malachi 3 and Hebrews 6 remind us of these truths:

Malachi 3: 16-18. "The Lord took note and listened, and a book of remembrance was written before him of those who revered the Lord and thought on his name. They shall be mine, says the Lord of hosts, my special possession on the day when I act, and I will spare them as parents spare their children who serve them. Then once more you shall see the difference between the righteous and the wicked, between one who serves God and one who does not serve him." NRSVCE

Hebrews 6: 9-12. "But we are sure in your regard, beloved, of better things related to salvation, even though we speak in this way. 10 For God is not unjust so as to overlook your work and the love you have demonstrated for his name by having served and continuing to serve the holy ones. 11 We earnestly desire each of you to demonstrate the same eagerness for the fulfillment of hope until the end, 12 so that you may not become sluggish, but imitators of those who, through faith and patience, are inheriting the promises." NABRE

7. ***REBUILDING WITH YOUR GIFTS.*** When Nehemiah was sent to rebuild the physical walls and gates, he was also rebuilding spiritual gates and walls. In the process, he used all the gifts God had given him. Now is a good time to ask God where the broken walls are in your life—spiritual or otherwise (including for yourself, your family and nation) and what gifts God has given you for the rebuilding work. Write down what comes to mind in the *Ponderings* below.

❖Ponderings

a. What gifts did God give Nehemiah?

b. What gifts God has given you to help you spiritually or physically rebuild your life, your family, your community and our nation?

c. How does God want to use your gifts now for rebuilding?

d. Nehemiah motivated others to help; who can you motivate or invite into rebuilding?

8. ***REFLECTION ON THIS CHAPTER.*** Please reflect on the principles that caught your attention from the work of rebuilding the walls and gates. Circle the ones that apply most to you and record what you can to start rebuilding today and why.

❖Ponderings

a. **I need to remember that Jesus is my *Sheep Gate.*** Though His Passion, death and resurrection for my sins. He paid the way and is my gate to eternal life. Thank you, Jesus.

b. **I need to allow the *Fish Gate*** to remind me to respond to Jesus' call to become a fisherman or fisherwoman. (In Matthew 4:18, Jesus speaks to me, "**Follow me, and I will make you fish for people**.")

c. **I can allow The *Old Gate*** to remind me the worth of renewing my commitment to the treasured faith of my Fathers. Jesus wants to renew me in that commitment. For the Lord never changes and "Jesus Christ is the same yesterday and today and forever" (Hebrews 13: 8).

d. **I can turn to God's comfort when I think of the *Valley Gate*** that reminds me when I am in a valley of desolation, overwhelmed by sin or darkness, I can look to Jesus, my Gate (John 10:8). He is always ready to comfort and forgive me. I can say with 2 Corinthians 1: 3-4, "Blessed be the God and Father of our Lord Jesus Christ, the Father of mercies and the God of all consolation, who consoles [me] in all [my] affliction, so that [I] may be able to console those who are in any affliction with the consolation with which [I am] consoled by God."

e. **I need to remind myself that I can use the *Dung Gate*** Jesus provides. Jesus is the one who can and will remove the sin garbage from my life through confession, repentance and His forgiveness. I can pray with 1 John 1: 7-10, "If [I] walk in the light as he himself is in the light, [I] have fellowship with one another, and the blood of Jesus his Son cleanses [me] from all sin. If [I] say that [I] have no sin, [I} deceive [myself], and the truth is not in [me]. If [I] confess [my] sins, he who is faithful and just will forgive [my] sins and cleanse [me] from all unrighteousness."

f. **I need to remember that the *Fountain Gate*** for me is Jesus, the *Fountain of Eternal Life.* I can pray with the words Jesus told the woman at the well: "Everyone who drinks of this water will be thirsty again, but [I} who drink of the water that Jesus gives [me] will never be thirsty. The water that Jesus gives will become in [me] a spring of water gushing up to eternal life" (John 4: 13-14). Jesus, you are my Fountain of Eternal Life!

g. **I need to look to the *Water Gate*** and remember to read the Word of God as water and healing for my soul. I will remember Basil the Great's words that the Scriptures are a "pharmacy of medicine" for my own illnesses and the Psalms are a "jewel case of remedies for all of my cases." With Psalm 1, I can pray: "Happy [I am] who does not follow the advice of the wicked, or take the path that sinners tread, or sit in the seat of scoffers; 2 but [my] delight is in the law of the Lord, and on his law [I] will meditate day and night. 3 [I will be] like a tree planted by streams of water, which yields fruit in its season, and [my] leaves do not wither. In all that [I} do, [I] will prosper," meaning I will have good return for my labors.

h. **I should remember the *Horse Gate,*** and the battle of spiritual warfare. Daily I need to dress myself with the armor of Ephesians 6: so that I might, "Stand and fasten the belt of truth around [my] waist, and put on the breastplate of righteousness. As shoes for [my] feet [I] put on whatever will make [me] ready to proclaim the gospel of peace. With all of these, [I] take the shield of faith, with which [I] will be able to quench all the flaming arrows of the evil one. Take the helmet of salvation, and the sword of the Spirit, which is the word of God. {I will] pray in the Spirit at all times in every prayer and … [I will] keep alert and always persevere in supplication..."

i. **I can remember the *East Gate,*** the first gate opened each morning, and remind myself of the importance of morning prayer. I can pray with Psalm 5: 3, "O Lord, in the morning you hear my voice; in the morning, I plead my case to you, and watch," and with Psalm 143: 8, "Let me hear of your steadfast love in the morning, for in you I put my trust."

j. **I need to recall the *Inspection Gate*** as a reminder to examine my conscience daily, to confess my sins and to receive the forgiveness of Jesus. I will pray with 1 John 1: 8-9, "If [I] say that [I] have no sin, [I] deceive [myself], and the truth is not in [me]. If [I] confess [my] sins, he who is faithful and just will forgive [me of my] sins and cleanse [me] from all unrighteousness." Also, I will be mindful of Acts 3: 19, {I will] repent … and turn to God so that [my] sins may be wiped out, so that times of refreshing may come from the presence of the Lord,

9. ***APPLICATION.*** Please record any burned down gates and broken walls in your life that need restoration. (Ask God where you have opened or "burned" gates that invite darkness into your life such as, sinful habits, addictions to alcohol, drugs, or cigarettes, uncontrolled imaginations, extreme fears, emotional hurts, lack of forgiveness, filthy television, internet or movies, pornography, unrestrained tongue, and generational sins) and broken walls, where you need increased strength, fortitude, faith, healing, persistence, or restoration. **Listen to God**—He may bring to your attention other gates or walls that need rebuilding. Ask for the tools and the hope to rebuild. Jesus wants to encourage you today.

❖Ponderings

a. Confess any sin and repent. Repentance involves a turn-round in direction. Consider where God wants to strengthen you and help you change attitudes of hopelessness, discouragement or procrastination, etc. Ask God what action you will take to confess, repent and turn from sin.

b. Where do you want to rebuild, but lack tools? Remember the perfumers and set your mind to build anyway. Ask God where to begin building and what you can do.

10. ***PERSONAL RAYER RESPONSE.*** Nehemiah has continued to teach us that no situation or brokenness is beyond God's help when we come to Him in intercessory prayer and faith. Now is a good time praying over the burned down gates and broken walls (especially spiritual gates and walls) that need repair in your life, your family, and your nation. Ask the Holy Spirit to guide you. Nehemiah models how to pray and intercede to our **Awesome** God summarized in the acronym ABCD (starting with D):

- **Declare** God's greatness and faithfulness with praises and Scripture,
- **Confess** our sins and those of our nation and families,
- **Believe** God and His Holy Word, and
- **Ask** for what you need and use Scripture, when possible.

Remember to spend a few minutes in silence asking God what He wants you to pray for yourself, your family or our nation. Now, prepare to intercede using the ABCD themes.

PREPARE FOR PRAYER

1) Write down your concerns.

MY CONCERNS, OPEN GATES, AND BROKENNESS this week INCLUDE:

2) Listen to the Holy Spirit who will guide you in prayer.

3) Recall God's greatness using scripture (see the Appendix for help with *Scriptures for Declaring God's Greatness* and *Praying with Confidence*).

4) Pray and write a summary of your prayer in the space on the next page.

MY INTERCESSORY PRAYER BASED ON NEHEMIAH 3: 1-38

- **D**eclare God's Greatness (with Scripture)

- **C**onfess the sins of your nation, your family, and yourself with the same passion as if indeed they all belonged to you.

- **B**elieve the truth of God's Word and His Faithfulness by recalling His blessings and the promises in Scripture (use those verses in prayer).

- **A**sk God for the needs He brings to mind. (Let the Holy Spirit lead you in prayer.)

5

PRAYER AND TEAMWORK

Connection Question

Have you ever faced ridicule, name-calling or a constant barrage of insults at school or work? If so, how did you respond?

People Working to Rebuild the Walls of Jerusalem[xxvii]

St. Takla.org

Nehemiah 4:15-23

Chapter 5: Prayer and Teamwork

Family by Family, Brick by Brick, House by House

In the last few weeks, we have read the Book of Nehemiah, a historical book and the 13th book in the Old Testament, written about a time beginning 445 BC. We joined Nehemiah, who after four months of prayer and fasting and the King's blessing, returned to repair the brokenness of the walls and rebuild the gates and the faith of the people in Jerusalem. God had put the desire in Nehemiah's heart and through intercession, opened the way for him to fulfill God's call to rebuild what had been destroyed and demoralized.

When Nehemiah arrived in Jerusalem, he secretly surveyed the broken walls and rubbish and then invited all to help rebuild the gates and stop the humiliation (2: 17). He encouraged the people that God's gracious favor was upon them and that the king had promised provision. "They replied, 'Let us begin building!' And they undertook the work with vigor" (2: 18, NABRE). However, once they started to rebuild, trouble arose. As can quickly happen when we focus on doing God's work, opposition can come with insults and derisions. This time it came from the leaders of the neighboring countries who meant to stop the rebuilding and demoralize the people.

Nehemiah answered the enemies of God's work and proclaimed: "The God of heaven is the one who will give us success, and we his servants are going to start building; but you have no share or claim or historic right in Jerusalem" (2: 20). So family-by-family and household-by-household and brick-by-brick, the people repaired the walls and rebuilt the gates near their properties and helped where neighbors would not or could not build. They worked side-by-side, beyond their own giftedness and vocations to do God's work and repair the walls and gates of their holy city.

Chapter Five Questions

1. ***NEHEMIAH 4.*** In preparation for this study, please read Nehemiah 4: 1- 23 and **circle** all the ways Nehemiah and the people faced the enemies and their accusations. Share what caught your attention.

Nehemiah 4: 1-23

Now when Sanballat heard that we were building the wall, he was angry and greatly
enraged, and he mocked the Jews. 2 He said in the presence of his associates and of the
army of Samaria, "What are these feeble Jews doing? Will they restore things? Will they
sacrifice? Will they finish it in a day? Will they revive the stones out of the heaps of
rubbish—and burned ones at that?" 3 Tobiah the Ammonite was beside him, and he said,
"That stone wall they are building—any fox going up on it would break it down!" 4 Hear,
O our God, for we are despised; turn their taunt back on their own heads, and give them
over as plunder in a land of captivity. 5 Do not cover their guilt, and do not let their sin be
blotted out from your sight; for they have hurled insults in the face of the builders.

6 So we rebuilt the wall, and all the wall was joined together to half its height; for the
people had a mind to work.

7 But when Sanballat and Tobiah and the Arabs and the Ammonites and the Ashdodites
heard that the repairing of the walls of Jerusalem was going forward and the gaps were
beginning to be closed, they were very angry, 8 and all plotted together to come and fight
against Jerusalem and to cause confusion in it. 9 So we prayed to our God, and set a guard
as a protection against them day and night.

10 But Judah said, "The strength of the burden bearers is failing, and there is too much
rubbish so that we are unable to work on the wall." 11 And our enemies said, "They will
not know or see anything before we come upon them and kill them and stop the work." 12
When the Jews who lived near them came, they said to us ten times, "From all the places
where they live they will come up against us." 13 So in the lowest parts of the space behind
the wall, in open places, I stationed the people according to their families, with their
swords, their spears, and their bows. 14 After I looked these things over, I stood up and
said to the nobles and the officials and the rest of the people, "Do not be afraid of them.
Remember the Lord, who is great and awesome, and fight for your kin, your sons, your
daughters, your wives, and your homes."

15 When our enemies heard that their plot was known to us, and that God had frustrated it,
we all returned to the wall, each to his work. 16 From that day on, half of my servants
worked on construction, and half held the spears, shields, bows, and body-armor; and the
leaders posted themselves behind the whole house of Judah, 17 who were building the
wall. The burden bearers carried their loads in such a way that each labored on the work
with one hand and with the other held a weapon. 18 And each of the builders had his
sword strapped at his side while he built. The man who sounded the trumpet was beside
me. 19 And I said to the nobles, the officials, and the rest of the people, "The work is great
and widely spread out, and we are separated far from one another on the wall. 20 Rally to
us wherever you hear the sound of the trumpet. Our God will fight for us."

21 So we labored at the work, and half of them held the spears from break of dawn until
the stars came out. 22 I also said to the people at that time, "Let every man and his servant
pass the night inside Jerusalem, so that they may be a guard for us by night and may labor
by day." 23 So neither I nor my brothers nor my servants nor the men of the guard who
followed me ever took off our clothes; each kept his weapon in his right hand.

2. ***ANGER NEXT DOOR*** (v. 1-2). When you read in Nehemiah 2:19 that Sanballet, the Governor of Samaria (**north** of Jerusalem), Tobiah, the leader from Ammon (**east** of Jerusalem), Geshem the leader of the Arabs (from Moab and Arabia, **east** and **south** of Jerusalem), and the men from Ashdod (v. 7) (**west** of Jerusalem) were coming together against Nehemiah and all Jerusalem, how bad would this possible attack look to the Jewish people?

❖Ponderings

a. Who was on Sanballat's side and what **weapons** did they use (v. 1-2)?

b. Why do you think their words were so demoralizing to the people? Read Deuteronomy 7: 1-6 to further answer this question.

Deuteronomy 7: 1-6. When the Lord your God brings you into the land that you are about to enter and occupy, and he clears away many nations before you—the Hittites, the Girgashites, the Amorites, the Canaanites, the Perizzites, the Hivites, and the Jebusites, seven nations mightier and more numerous than you— 2 and when the Lord your God gives them over to you and you defeat them, then you must utterly destroy them. Make no covenant with them and show them no mercy. 3 Do not intermarry with them, giving your daughters to their sons or taking their daughters for your sons, 4 for that would turn away your children from following me, to serve other gods. Then the anger of the Lord would be kindled against you, and he would destroy you quickly. 5 But this is how you must deal with them: break down their altars, smash their pillars, hew down their sacred poles, and burn their idols with fire. 6 For you are a people holy to the Lord your God; the Lord your God has chosen you out of all the peoples on earth to be his people, his treasured possession. NRSVCE

3. ***SURROUNDED BY TROUBLE*** (v. 4-6). According to v. 4-6, how did Nehemiah respond to the opposition surrounding them?

❖Ponderings

a. How did the prayer show his feistiness?

b. Were the people encouraged by Nehemiah's prayer?

4. ***SUCCESS AND MORE OPPOSITION*** (v. 6-8). How far did the builders get and how did they accomplish this feat (v. 6)?

❖Ponderings

a. How was the opposition ramped up (v. 7-8)?

b. How would you describe Nehemiah's two-pronged approach and his confidence (v. 9)?

5. ***NEHEMIAH'S STRATEGY FOR PROBLEMS*** (v. 10-14). In the space below, list the major problems that arose?

- From within (v. 10)
- From the Enemy (v. 11)?
- From the Jews who lived near the enemy territories (v. 12)?

❖Ponderings

a. How would you describe Nehemiah's approach and confidence (v. 13-14)?

b. What made Nehemiah's words so encouraging to the people (v. 14)?

6. ***POSTING GUARD*** (v. 15). What happens when the Jewish people return to work?

❖Ponderings

a. How did the people support and help each other? (v. 16-20)

b. What did Nehemiah have them do at night? (v. 21-23)

c. In the space below, fill in the opposition's response and Nehemiah's offensive response:

- **Nehemiah 4: 1-6**
  - The Opposition's (v. 1-3) Ridicule and mockery:
  - Nehemiah's Offensive Response (v. 4-6) Prayer and hard work:

- **Nehemiah 4: 7-23**
  - The Opposition's (v. 1-3) Intimidation, plots, and threats of physical violence
  - Nehemiah's Offensive Response (v. 4-6): Prayer, hard work and posting of guard and trumpeter

d. What do you notice about Nehemiah's wording that shows how a good defense against opposition can turn into the best offense?

The Enemies Heckled, Nehemiah Prayed and the People Worked Together

In this chapter, we saw how the enemies heckled the rebuilding process. Sanballat and Tobiah mocked the builders and told them how hopeless they were because they used old worn-out materials— stones that had been burned, destroyed, cracked and crumbled by fire. Thus, they taunted the stones for the walls could not be revived. **That's sound just like the devil. He loves to taunt us even to this day with** discouragement, disbelief, distrust, ridicule or oppression to keep each of us from progressing, working together and listening to the Holy Spirit.

We can remind ourselves of John 14: 25-27, "I have said these things to you while I am still with you. [26] But the Advocate, the Holy Spirit, whom the Father will send in my name, will teach you everything, and remind you of all that I have said to you. [27] Peace I leave with you; my peace I give to you. I do not give to you as the world gives. **Do not let your hearts be troubled, and do not let them be afraid."** You are in charge of your own soul (i.e., you are the governor) and you can choose to take spiritual control of any discouragement and ridicule. Be sure to join others in the process. Remember, God can use the old, cracked and warn out tools. John 4: 4 reminds us, "the one who is in you [the Holy Spirit] is greater than he who is in the world.

7. ***REFLECTION.*** When Nehemiah was sent to repair the physical walls and rebuild the gates, he was also rebuilding spiritual gates. As you study Nehemiah, please ask God where the broken gates are in your life—spiritual or otherwise - and what **weapons** you can use to fight the opposition against your rebuilding efforts?

❖Ponderings

a. Write down all the broken gates in your life that need restoration and where your life needs strength, faith repentance, restoration, healing and separation from attitudes of the worldly culture?

b. What **spiritual weapons has God given you** to fight discouragement while you work to rebuild the gates in your life, your family, and your nation?

c. What three things did Nehemiah ask the people to do in v. 13-14?

d. Read Proverbs 4: 13-15 and 4: 23-27, and circle what you can do to stand guard over your own spiritual life.

Proverbs 4: 13-15. Keep hold of instruction; do not let go; guard her, for she
is your life. 14 Do not enter the path of the wicked, and do not walk in the
way of evildoers. 15 Avoid it; do not go on it; turn away from it and pass on.

Proverbs 4: 23-27. Keep your heart with all vigilance, for from it flow the
springs of life. 24 Put away from you crooked speech, and put devious talk far
from you. 25 Let your eyes look directly forward, and your gaze be straight
before you. 26 Keep straight the path of your feet, and all your ways will be
sure. 27 Do not swerve to the right or to the left; turn your foot away from
evil.

8. ***APPLICATION.*** Consider any rubbish in your life. What **action** can you take to restore the broken gates you listed in #7? Consider what you learn from Nehemiah that can help you rebuild your burned down gates?

❖Ponderings

a. Rubbish. Where is the rubbish (v. 10) in your life that God wants to remove, such as 1) an unforgiving spirit; 2) bitterness's and anger over troubles that have befallen you like bad health, job loss, financial insecurity, marital and family issues; 3) useless fear, worry and anxiety over things we cannot seem to control; 4) painful and hurtful memories; 5) confusion about where to turn for help—a feeling of discouragement, etc. The evil one will try to influence your life so these things burden you just as he tried for the people at Nehemiah's time ("The strength of the burden-bearers is failing, and there is too much rubbish so that we are unable to work on the wall (v. 10)." List the rubbish in your life that needs to be removed in order for you to LIVE the Lord's plan for your life?

b. What gates do you continue to open that lets the rubbish in?

9. ***ACTIONS.*** Nehemiah commanded his people to fight for their families and to take three actions. What actions will you take to remove the rubbish?

a. The Team. Who is on your team to help with the rebuilding? Where can you find the teamwork to help hold up your spiritual weapons and prayer with you?

b. Spiritual Weapons. How will you overcome any opposition that greets you? Insults? Half-truths? Lies? Mocking? Read Ephesians 6: 10-18 and circle all the spiritual weapons that you can hold in your hands while you remove the rubbish in your life?

Ephesians 6: 10-18. Finally, be strong in the Lord and in the strength of his power. 11
Put on the whole armor of God, so that you may be able to stand against the wiles of
the devil. 12 For our struggle is not against enemies of blood and flesh, but against the
rulers, against the authorities, against the cosmic powers of this present darkness,
against the spiritual forces of evil in the heavenly places. 13 Therefore take up the
whole armor of God, so that you may be able to withstand on that evil day, and
having done everything, to stand firm. 14 Stand therefore, and fasten the belt of truth
around your waist, and put on the breastplate of righteousness. 15 As shoes for your
feet put on whatever will make you ready to proclaim the gospel of peace. 16 With all
of these, take the shield of faith, with which you will be able to quench all the
flaming arrows of the evil one. 17 Take the helmet of salvation, and the sword of the
Spirit, which is the word of God. 18 Pray in the Spirit at all times in every prayer and
supplication. To that end keep alert and always persevere in supplication for all the
saints.

c. Scripture. Are you letting the Word of God strengthen you daily? Reread and pray Nehemiah 4: 14.

   i. Insert your name in Nehemiah's prayer and then the names of your friends and family members. For example, see the following.

      "Do not be afraid of them. Remember the Lord, who is great and awesome, and [I will] fight for [my] kin, [my] sons, [my] daughters, [my] wives, and [my] home."

   ii. Reread and declare aloud the last part of v. 20 and pray this often.

      "Our God will fight for us." My God will fight for my family, my community and my country."

   iii. Where do you need support? Ask someone to pray with you for your needs and you pray for their needs.

10. ***PERSONAL PRAYER RESPONSE.*** Nehemiah has taught us to pray, repent and take action with prayer and faith. Now the Lord wants to lead you in prayer. Nehemiah models how to intercede to our **Awesome** God summarized in the acronym ABCD (starting with D):

- **Declare** God's greatness and faithfulness with praises and Scripture,

- **Confess** our sins and those of our nation and families,

- **Believe** God and His Holy Word, and

- **Ask** for what you need and use Scripture, when possible.

Please review Nehemiah 4: 1-23 and especially to your answers to questions #7, #8 and #9. Then prepare to intercede for yourself, your family and your nation referring to your answers in #7, #8 and #9 and using the ABCD themes.

PREPARE FOR PRAYER

1) Write down your concerns.

MY CONCERNS AND/OR OPEN GATES WHERE RUBBISH COMES IN:

2) Listen to the Holy Spirit who will guide you in prayer.

3) Recall God's greatness using scripture (see the Appendix for help with *Scriptures for Declaring God's Greatness* and *Praying with Confidence*).

4) Pray and write a summary of your prayer in the space on the next page.

MY INTECESSORY PRAYER BASED ON NEHEMIAH 4: 1 - 23

- **D**eclare God's Greatness (with Scripture)

- **C**onfess the sins of your nation, your family, and yourself with the same passion as if indeed they all belonged to you.

- **B**elieve the truth of God's Word and His Faithfulness by recalling His blessings and the promises in Scripture (use those verses in prayer).

- **A**sk God for the needs He brings to mind. (Let the Holy Spirit lead you in prayer.)

6

GODLY LEADERSHIP

Connection Question

How much do financial burdens add to already hard times of great stress or mental exhaustion?

Nehemiah Rebukes the Nobles and Rulers
for Exacting Usury from Their Brethren[xxviii]
St. Takla. Org
Nehemiah 5: 7-13

Chapter Six - Godly Leadership

Fight for Your Families

In the last few weeks of our study, we joined Nehemiah in Persia, who after four months of prayer and fasting and the King's blessing, returned to rebuild the brokenness of the walls, the gates, and the people in Jerusalem. God put the desire in Nehemiah's heart and through intercessory prayer opened the way for him to return to his beloved city to rebuild what had been destroyed and demoralized. In Jerusalem, Nehemiah found much brokenness and despair. After inspecting the city at night and encountering the ruins, he encouraged the people that God's favor was with them and so they "strengthened their hands for the good work" (2: 18).

Once God's people started to rebuild, insults and derisions came from the leaders of the neighboring countries, who tried to stop the rebuilding and demoralize the people. Nehemiah answered them: **"The God of heaven is the one who will give us success, and we his servants are going to start building; but you have no share or claim or historic right to Jerusalem** (2: 20)." So family-by-family and household-by-household, the people worked side-by-side, beyond their own giftedness and vocations, to rebuild the walls and gates of their holy city. When greater persecution came, Nehemiah prayed first and then called his people to stand guard at the gates, to work in teams, and to rebuild with a weapon for warfare in one hand and bricks in the other. The rebuilding project was looking good thanks to the faithfulness of God, the leadership of Nehemiah and the great participation of the people.

Today, we join Nehemiah as he responds to an outcry from the people. The immoral and religiously unlawful practices of some had put the families in poverty and their children in slavery. So Nehemiah called an assembly and confronted the nobles and officials with their ungodly moneylending, interest charging, and then the selling of their children into slavery. He demanded they all return to God's lawful practices or lose their possessions in God' justice. The people responded, "Amen," and praised the Lord.

Chapter Six Questions

1. ***NEHEMIAH 5: 1- 19.*** In preparation for this study, please read Nehemiah 5: 1–19 and **circle** the outcry and complaints of the people. Share what caught your attention in these verses.

Nehemiah 5: 1-19

Now there was a great outcry of the people and of their wives against their Jewish kin. 2 For there were those who said, "With our sons and our daughters, we are many; we must get grain, so that we may eat and stay alive." 3 There were also those who said, "We are having to pledge our fields, our vineyards, and our houses in order to get grain during the famine." 4 And there were those who said, "We are having to borrow money on our fields and vineyards to pay the king's tax. 5 Now our flesh is the same as that of our kindred; our children are the same as their children; and yet we are forcing our sons and daughters to be slaves, and some of our daughters have been ravished; we are powerless, and our fields and vineyards now belong to others."

I was very angry when I heard their outcry and these complaints. 7 After thinking it over, I brought charges against the nobles and the officials; I said to them, "You are all taking interest from your own people." And I called a great assembly to deal with them, 8 and said to them, "As far as we were able, we have bought back our Jewish kindred who had been sold to other nations; but now you are selling your own kin, who must then be bought back by us!" They were silent, and could not find a word to say. 9 So I said, "The thing that you are doing is not good. Should you not walk in the fear of our God, to prevent the taunts of the nations, our enemies? 10 Moreover I and my brothers and my servants are lending them money and grain. Let us stop this taking of interest. 11 Restore to them, this very day, their fields, their vineyards, their olive orchards, and their houses, and the interest on money, grain, wine, and oil that you have been exacting from them." 12 Then they said, "We will restore everything and demand nothing more from them. We will do as you say." And I called the priests, and made them take an oath to do as they had promised. 13 I also shook out the fold of my garment and said, "So may God shake out everyone from house and from property who does not perform this promise. Thus, may they be shaken out and emptied." And all the assembly said, "Amen," and praised the Lord. And the people did as they had promised.

14 Moreover from the time that I was appointed to be their governor in the land of Judah, from the twentieth year to the thirty-second year of King Artaxerxes, twelve

years, neither I nor my brothers ate the food allowance of the governor. 15 The former
governors who were before me laid heavy burdens on the people, and took food and
wine from them, besides forty shekels of silver. Even their servants lorded it over the
people. But I did not do so, because of the fear of God. 16 Indeed, I devoted myself to
the work on this wall, and acquired no land; and all my servants were gathered
there for the work. 17 Moreover there were at my table one hundred fifty people,
Jews and officials, besides those who came to us from the nations around us. 18 Now
that which was prepared for one day was one ox and six choice sheep; also fowls
were prepared for me, and every ten days skins of wine in abundance; yet with all
this I did not demand the food allowance of the governor, because of the heavy
burden of labor on the people. 19 Remember for my good, O my God, all that I have
done for this people. NRSVCE

2. ***THE OUTCRY*** (v. 5: 2-6). In the space below, please list the people who have an outcry and the subject matter of their complaints from Nehemiah 5: 2-5.

The People	Their Outcries and Complaints
i. –	
ii. –	
iii. –	

❖**Ponderings**

a. What example shows how bad their poverty had become (v. 5)?

b. How did they feel? (See v. 5: "We are ____________, and our fields and vineyards now belong to others.")

c. What was Nehemiah's response to hearing their outcry?

d. What do you learn from Nehemiah's wise response in v. 6?

Poverty

Inflation had become rampant for many at this time. The Persian King had taken much of the monetary coins out of circulation as taxes so the coins could be melted down and stored as silver or gold. Also, the nobles acquired land, which removed it from production, and thus food prices had risen for the Jewish people by as much as 50%. In order to pay the taxes, it seems that the families under duress would borrow money from others using their own children as collateral. Thus, if loans could not be repaid, their children and even the wives and husbands, would be sold into bondage or taken as slaves. Fortunately, the law found in Leviticus 25: 39-40 and Deuteronomy 15: 12-18 said that any Israelite who had been sold into slavery should be released in the seventh year:

> **Leviticus 25: 39-41.** If any who are dependent on you become so impoverished that they sell themselves to you, you shall not make them serve as slaves. 40 They shall remain with you as hired or bound laborers. They shall serve with you until the year of the jubilee. 41 Then they and their children with them shall be free from your authority; they shall go back to their own family and return to their ancestral property.

> **Deuteronomy 15: 12-15.** If a member of your community, whether a Hebrew man or a Hebrew woman, is sold to you and works for you six years, in the seventh year you shall set that person free. 13 And when you send a male slave out from you a free person, you shall not send him out empty-handed. 14 Provide liberally out of your flock, your threshing floor, and your wine press, thus giving to him some of the bounty with which the Lord your God has blessed you. 15 Remember that you were a slave in the land of Egypt, and the Lord your God redeemed you; for this reason I lay this command upon you today.

The morale of the people was already very low because of the many hindrances and threats from their enemies. The stress on the people was compounded with physical exhaustion, lack of food, and the financial crisis. Their problems and troubles were overwhelming. They needed to be reminded of who they were as God's people, and the laws they must follow.

3. ***RESTITUTION*** (v. 7-14). What charges did Nehemiah make and to whom (v. 7)?

❖Ponderings

a. What three demands did Nehemiah make and why were they so important (v. 8-10)?

b. What do think Nehemiah's symbolic response to their oath meant (v. 12-13)?

The Symbolism of the Gesture and Response to the Oath

Nehemiah protested the actions of the nobles and the officials who were extracting the interest and enslaving their own brethren and children. He called them to repent (change directions) and 1) walk in fear or reverence of God, 2) stop taking interest and 3) restore everything that had been taken. Then the officials gave him their oath.

In one dramatic display symbolizing the importance and solemnity of the oath, Nehemiah shook out the fold of his garment and said, "So may God shake out everyone from house and from property who does not perform this promise. Thus, may they be shaken out and emptied." In this, he emphasized that judgment would come to those who did not keep their oath before God. The assembly confirmed it with a passionate "Amen." They "praised the Lord…and "did as they had promised."

4. ***THE GOVERNOR*** (5: 14). What did you learn about Nehemiah in v. 14?

❖Ponderings

a. How would you describe Nehemiah as the governor compared to the ones before him or the other nobles and leaders (v. 15-17)?

b. How did he help his people (v. 18)?

Note. Nehemiah was the Governor for 12 Years (v. 14) could have been an insertion by Nehemiah in his memoirs to emphasize his sacrifice in service to his people. The previous governors (indicated in archeological evidence from Jerusalem coins.xxix) would use food and land allotments demanded from the people in order to support their own palaces, but Nehemiah used his own money earned as cupbearer to the king of Persia. He chose to use his own wealth to support the poor and suffering people of Jerusalem instead of gaining financial opportunity from his position.

5. ***REVERENCING GOD.*** Nehemiah demonstrates how to reverence God, use authority and inspire others in his actions—even in the midst of adversity, moral decline and corruption. Please ponder his responses in the following situations and circle the ones that most challenge you.

   a. Nehemiah became very angry (v. 6), but did not immediately act on his anger. Instead, he thought it through and discerned God's response before taking action (v. 7).

   b. Nehemiah approached the corrupt moneylending by calling the officials back to God and asking them to follow God's Law—The Word of God (v. 9).

   c. Nehemiah showed how to come to the aid of his brethren by lending them what they needed and not taking interest (v. 10-11).

   d. Nehemiah pointed out the consequences of breaking the oath to God and returning to the immoral money lending practices and enslaving the poor (v. 12-13).

   e. Nehemiah, out of reverence for God, used his authority and wealth to help his people (v. 10, 14-18).

6. ***ADVERSITY.*** When Nehemiah was sent to rebuild the physical gates and walls (as well as spiritual faith), he faced much adversity. Please ask God where the broken gates are in your life and what you can learn from Nehemiah about facing adversity?

❖Ponderings

a. **The Gates:** Ask God again to help you see the **open gates and broken walls in your life that need restoration** (Where does your life need strength? Faith? Repentance? Healing? Restoration from hopelessness? Separation from attitudes of our worldly culture?). Now **write down the spiritual gates in your life that need to be rebuilt in faith.**

b. **The Adversity.** Nehemiah prayed that God would strengthen their hands (v. 6: 9). Where do you need God to strengthen your hands? Where do you need comfort and help in facing adversity? Where are your enemies intimidating you? Now **write down the adversity you face and ask God for his powerful help**

7. ***APPLICATION- HANDLING ADVERSITY.*** Ask God what to do with the adversity and enemies that come against you? Begin by praying with these Scriptures.
   a. Circle the ones that seem most pertinent to you and pray them back to the Lord.

Joshua 1:9. I hereby command you: Be strong and courageous; do not be frightened or dismayed, for the Lord your God is with you wherever you go." Your Prayer:

Psalm 27: 1. The Lord is my light and my salvation; whom shall I fear? The Lord is the stronghold of my life; of whom shall I be afraid? Your Prayer:

Isaiah 41: 13. For I, the Lord your God, hold your right hand; it is I who say to you, "Do not fear, I will help you." Your Prayer:

Proverbs 3: 5-6. Trust in the Lord with all your heart, and do not rely on your own insight. [6] In all your ways acknowledge him, and he will make straight your paths. Your Prayer:

Proverbs 12: 25. Anxiety weighs down the human heart, but a good word cheers it up. Your Prayer:

Romans 12: 1-2. I appeal to you therefore, brothers and sisters, by the mercies of God, to present your bodies as a living sacrifice, holy and acceptable to God, which is your spiritual worship. [2] Do not be conformed to this world, but be transformed by the renewing of your minds, so that you may discern what is the will of God—what is good and acceptable and perfect. Your Prayer:

Philippians 4: 6-7. [D]do not be anxious about anything, but in everything by prayer and supplication with thanksgiving let your requests be made known to God. And the peace of God, which surpasses all understanding, will guard your hearts and your minds in Christ Jesus. Your Prayer:

James 1: 19-21. Know this, my dear brothers: everyone should be quick to hear, slow to speak, slow to, [20] for the wrath of a man does not accomplish the righteousness of God. [21] Therefore, put away all filth and evil excess and humbly welcome the word that has been planted in you and is able to save your souls. NABRE Your Prayer:

b. Now write down the steps you will take to overcome the adversity.

8. ***PERSONAL PRAYER RESPONSE.*** Nehemiah has taught us that no opposition is beyond God's hand of deliverance when we come to Him in prayer and faith. God wants to lead YOU. Nehemiah models how to pray and intercede to our **Awesome** God summarized in the acronym ABCD (starting with D):

- **Declare** God's greatness and faithfulness with praises and Scripture,
- **Confess** our sins and those of our nation and families,
- **Believe** God and His Holy Word, and
- **Ask** for what you need and use Scripture, when possible.

Remember to spend a few minutes in silence asking God what He wants you to pray for yourself, your family or our nation. Now, prepare to intercede using the ABCD themes.

PREPARE FOR PRAYER

1) Write down your concerns.

MY CONCERNS, OPEN GATES, AND BROKENNESS this week INCLUDE:

2) Listen to the Holy Spirit who will guide you in prayer.

3) Recall God's greatness using scripture (see the Appendix for help with *Scriptures for Declaring God's Greatness* and *Praying with Confidence*).

4) Pray and write a summary of your prayer in the space on the next page.

MY INTERCESSORY PRAYER BASED ON NEHEMIAH 5: 1-17

- **D**eclare God's Greatness (with Scripture)

- **C**onfess the sins of your nation, your family, and yourself with the same passion as if indeed they all belonged to you.

- **B**elieve the truth of God's Word and His Faithfulness by recalling His blessings and the promises in Scripture (use those verses in prayer).

- **A**sk God for the needs He brings to mind. (Let the Holy Spirit lead you in prayer.)

7

FACING THE ENEMY

Connection Question

Have others ever spread a lie or untrue rumor about you?
How did you feel and what did you do?

Sanballat and Geshem Send a Message to Nehemiah
Asking to Meet with Him[xxx]
St. Takla.Org
Nehemiah 6: 2-3

Chapter Seven - Facing the Enemy

Repentance and an Oath

In our last session, Nehemiah responded to an outcry from the people. The immoral and unlawful practices (based on God's commands) of the Jewish nobles and officials brought many families to poverty and caused their children to be enslaved. So Nehemiah called an assembly and confronted the officials with their ungodly money lending and interest charging, along with the selling of the children into slavery. He demanded they return to following God's laws, or as a consequence they would lose their possessions in God' justice. The Jewish officials made an oath to do this and responded, "Amen," and "praised the Lord."

Today, we join the Israelites as the wall repairs are completed, but the enemies from surrounding countries become fearful about losing their authority and illicit moneymaking practices. Thus, inspired by evil, they use conspiracy, personal attacks on Nehemiah, character assassination, threats, and even hire a false prophet to lure Nehemiah into sin.

Chapter Seven Questions

1. ***CONNECTION.*** In preparation for this study, please read Nehemiah 6: 1-19 and **circle** the names of all the enemies and their schemes. Share what you learn about the enemies their evil tactics on Nehemiah.

Nehemiah 6: 1-19

Now when it was reported to Sanballat and Tobiah and to Geshem the Arab and to
the rest of our enemies that I had built the wall and that there was no gap left in it
(though up to that time I had not set up the doors in the gates), 2 Sanballat and
Geshem sent to me, saying, "Come and let us meet together in one of the villages in
the plain of Ono." But they intended to do me harm. 3 So I sent messengers to them,
saying, "I am doing a great work and I cannot come down. Why should the work
stop while I leave it to come down to you?" 4 They sent to me four times in this way,
and I answered them in the same manner. 5 In the same way Sanballat for the fifth
time sent his servant to me with an open letter in his hand. 6 In it was written, "It is
reported among the nations—and Geshem also says it—that you and the Jews intend
to rebel; that is why you are building the wall; and according to this report you wish
to become their king. 7 You have also set up prophets to proclaim in Jerusalem
concerning you, 'There is a king in Judah!' And now it will be reported to the king
according to these words. So come, therefore, and let us confer together." 8 Then I
sent to him, saying, "No such things as you say have been done; you are inventing
them out of your own mind" 9 —for they all wanted to frighten us, thinking, "Their
hands will drop from the work, and it will not be done." But now, O God, strengthen
my hands.

10 One day when I went into the house of Shemaiah son of Delaiah son of Mehetabel,
who was confined to his house, he said, "Let us meet together in the house of God,
within the temple, and let us close the doors of the temple, for they are coming to kill
you; indeed, tonight they are coming to kill you." 11 But I said, "Should a man like
me run away? Would a man like me go into the temple to save his life? I will not go
in!" 12 Then I perceived and saw that God had not sent him at all, but he had
pronounced the prophecy against me because Tobiah and Sanballat had hired him.
13 He was hired for this purpose, to intimidate me and make me sin by acting in this
way, and so they could give me a bad name, in order to taunt me. 14 Remember
Tobiah and Sanballat, O my God, according to these things that they did, and also
the prophetess Noadiah and the rest of the prophets who wanted to make me afraid.

The Wall Completed

15 So the wall was finished on the twenty-fifth day of the month Elul*, in fifty-two
days.16 And when all our enemies heard of it, all the nations around us were afraid
and fell greatly in their own esteem; for they perceived that this work had been
accomplished with the help of our God. 17 Moreover in those days the nobles of
Judah sent many letters to Tobiah, and Tobiah's letters came to them. 18 For many in
Judah were bound by oath to him, because he was the son-in-law of Shecaniah son of
Arah: and his son Jehohanan had married the daughter of Meshullam son of
Berechiah. 19 Also they spoke of his good deeds in my presence, and reported my
words to him. And Tobiah sent letters to intimidate me.

***Note.** The twenty-fifth day of Elul was October 2, 444 BC.

2. ***ATTACK 1: THE SCHEME FOR A FRIENDLY MEETING*** (v. 1-5). Who sent Nehemiah a letter in v. 1 and what was wrong with the peace proposal?

❖Ponderings

a. What did Nehemiah discern was the real purpose for their supposedly friendly meeting (v. 2) and how did he respond (v. 3)?

b. How much pressure did the enemies put on Nehemiah (v. 4.-5)?

c. How did Nehemiah have such good discernment (being able to see things from God's point of view)?

d. Why is it important to prayerfully discern the many invitations or requests that sound good or godly or friendly, but could distract you from focusing on what God has called you to do—your true priorities?

Discerning the Friendly Meeting Scheme

The work on the wall had progressed beyond expectation and it was almost finished at this time—only the gates had yet to be installed. Obviously, this was the last chance for the enemies to stop the project. They would try anything. The first thing they tried was to arrange for a friendly, peace meeting in the hills of Ono (at least a full-day journey away and on the far western side of Jerusalem, where the returning Israelites had settled—it is near Tel Aviv today). It sounded like a neutral place, but Nehemiah discerned it as a scheme to do him harm (v. 2). The enemies pressured Nehemiah four times, but he responded that he was too busy building something great. He was strong in his priorities and focus on what God had called him to do. His faithfulness to a strong prayer life and to the Word of God (God's laws) helped him discern the harm they planned in what looked like a nice get-together Jesus words in Matthew 10:16 on discerning evil speak to us today: "See, I am sending you out like sheep into the midst of wolves; so be wise as serpents and innocent as doves."

2. **ATTACK 2: DESTROY HIS REPUTATION:** What was their scheme in the unsealed letter (v. 6-8)?

    a. How did Nehemiah respond to the made-up lies, slander and threats (v. 8-9)?

    b. What were their lies?

    c. How did Nehemiah know when to say no (v. 9)?

    d. How is slander one of devil's big weapons to stop God's work?

    e. When you face threats and slander, what can you do?

Discerning Slander and Responding to Threats

Next, in an unsealed letter, Sanballat told Nehemiah that the nations were talking about his treasonous plot to revolt and overthrow the King of Persia. Obviously, by not sealing the letter, Sanballat knew that others would read the contents and the lies would be spread everywhere—it was a scheme from hell that had worked twenty years prior (when the King shut down the rebuilding efforts because of treasonous rumors—see Chapter 2). Nehemiah replied that they were out of their mind and they "all wanted to frighten us, thinking, 'Their hands will drop from the work, and it will not be done.'" ("The hands will drop from their work" was a Hebrew idiom, meaning they will be too discouraged to keep working.) Again, Nehemiah did what he knew to do when he faced difficult and fearful circumstances, lies, accusations, deception or persecution: Stay focus and pray. So he prayed: "But now, O God, strengthen my hands." Nehemiah was determined not to let what others say curtail what God had given him to do.

3. **ATTACK 3: FALSE PROPHECY AND A RELIGIOUS MOLE**. What was the false prophecy of Shemaiah and who hired him (v. 10, 12)?

   a. How did the enemy use spiritual deception to tempt Nehemiah?

   b. What did Nehemiah discern would happen if he took refuge in the temple (e.g., Numbers 18: 6-7 shows the sin Nehemiah chose to avoid)?

      Numbers 18:6-7. It is I [God] who now take your brother **Levites** from among the Israelites…dedicated to the Lord, to perform the service of the tent of meeting… but any outsider who approaches shall be put to death.

   c. How does a knowledge of God's Word and His ways, keep you from spiritual deception or compromise that leads to sin?

4. **WALL COMPLETED** (v. 15-16). How long did it take to complete the wall and what impact did the completion of the wall have on the enemies (v. 16)?

❖Ponderings

a. How was it possible to repair the wall so quickly when it lay in ruins so long?

b. How had Tobiah gained authority and influence in Israel?

Nehemiah 6: 16. "All the nations around us were afraid...for they perceived that this work had been accomplished with the help of our God." NRSVCE

Discerning What God Says

Tobiah and Sanballat hired Shemaiah to intimidate Nehemiah, mislead him and get him to commit a sin of hiding in the temple holy place, which was reserved for priests by Jewish Law. (For example, when King Uzziah went into the temple to make an offering, as described in 2 Chronicles 26: 19, he was struck with leprosy because he violated the Jewish Law that said only priests could enter the temple and make an offering). Shemaiah tried to use tales of terror and "religious speak," like "house of God" and "let us close the doors of the temple because they are coming to kill you." Nehemiah had prayed and God had given him discernment to see the sinful trap of entering the temple when he was not a priest. If he had gone into the temple, it would have been a sin the enemies would use to discredit him and give him a "bad name."

God blessed Nehemiah, answered his prayers and helped the Israelites complete the wall in only 52 days. This was a great victory for the people because in the past they had accomplished so little over the many years because of their discouragement and opposition from the same enemies. But Nehemiah led the way, gave them new hope in God and encouraged them to work together.

Many in Judah "were under oath" to Tobiah (v. 18) because of family ties or financial contracts. They became blinded to the evil Tobiah committed. They lacked the discernment that comes from seeking God in prayer, His Word and His ways. Thus, they repeatedly reported to Nehemiah the "good deeds" Tobiah did, but Tobiah kept sending "letters to intimidate" Nehemiah (v. 19).

5. ***STENGTHENED.*** Nehemiah prayed that God would strengthen their hands (v. 9). Where do your hands and your life need to be strengthened?

❖Ponderings

a. Where are your enemies (physical or spiritual) intimidating you? Where is Satan using the enemies to tempt you with sin?

b. Often the hardest attack comes just prior to a victory? What does Hebrews 10: 35-39 teach you about prayerful persistence?

Hebrews 10: 35-39. Do not, therefore, abandon that confidence of yours; it brings a great reward. [36] For you need endurance, so that when you have done the will of God, you may receive what was promised. [37] For yet "in a very little while, the one who is coming will come and will not delay; [38] but my righteous one will live by faith. My soul takes no pleasure in anyone who shrinks back." [39] But we are not among those who shrink back and so are lost, but among those who have faith and so are saved.

6. ***PRIORITIES.*** Nehemiah had priorities. He set his mind and heart on finishing the wall. What could you do if you had your mind set on getting something done for God?

❖Ponderings

a. What would it take for you to set priorities and focus?

b. Ask God what priorities He would like you to start focusing on today and write them down here.

7. ***TACTICS OF EVIL.*** Fr. Louis Cameli in his *book The Devil You Don't Know - Recognizing and Resisting Evil in Everyday Life* says the devil's tactics always include: 1) discouragement, 2) division, 3) diversion from your primary goal and 4) deception.[xxxi] Where do you see these tactics in the schemes of the enemies targeting Nehemiah?

❖Ponderings

a. Which of these four tactics are targeting you?

b. The Devil always lies by suggesting thoughts such as: *God does not care. God is too small. God cannot help. You need to take things into your own hands. You cannot trust God. You can do it yourself.* When a person stops trusting, takes things into his/her own hands, stops working with God, allows holes in the walls and opens gates to evil, and then goes back to former sins, what is happening? What can you do?

c. What does Jesus say in John 8: 44 about the tactics of the devil?

John 8: 44. You are from your father the devil, and you choose to do your father's desires. He was a murderer from the beginning and does not stand in the truth, because there is no truth in him. When he lies, he speaks according to his own nature, for he is a liar and the father of lies.

8. ***WEAKNESS.*** Nehemiah worked for cooperation. It could have been his weakest area, if he did not discern where evil was trying to enter in a peace treaty proposal. Where is your weakest area? Pray Romans 16: 25 and Colossians 1: 9-14, asking Jesus to strengthen you in your weakest areas.

Romans 16: 25. "Now to God who is able to strengthen you according to my gospel and the proclamation of Jesus Christ, according to the revelation of the mystery that was kept secret for long ages. Amen." My Prayer:

Colossians 1: 9. "For this reason, since the day we heard it, we have not ceased praying for you and asking that you may be filled with the knowledge of God's will in all spiritual wisdom and understanding, [10] so that you may lead lives worthy of the Lord, fully pleasing to him, as you bear fruit in every good work and as you grow in the knowledge of God. [11] May you be made strong with all the strength that comes from his glorious power, and may you be prepared to endure everything with patience, while joyfully [12] giving thanks to the Father, who has enabled you to share in the inheritance of the saints in the light. [13] He has rescued us from the power of darkness and transferred us into the kingdom of his beloved Son, [14] in whom we have redemption, the forgiveness of sins." My Prayer:

9. ***APPLICATION.*** Nehemiah remained faithful to God through much opposition of scheming, persecution and accusations from the enemies. What have your learned from these Scriptures about facing your enemies?

   a. What did Nehemiah show you about responding to false accusations or evil schemes?

   b. What does Romans 12: 19-21 add to your actions for facing enemies?

Romans 12: 19-21. Beloved, never avenge yourselves, but leave room for the wrath of God; for it is written, "Vengeance is mine, I will repay, says the Lord." [20] No, "if your enemies are hungry, feed them; if they are thirsty, give them something to drink; for by doing this you will heap burning coals on their heads." [21] Do not be overcome by evil, but overcome evil with good.

Watchful

If we are prayerful, watching our gates for letting in evil and asking the Lord to help defend us against evil, He will! Psalm 121: 3- 8 reminds us of His protection:

> **Psalm 121: 3-8.** He will not let your foot be moved; he who keeps you will not slumber. 4 He who keeps Israel will neither slumber nor sleep. 5 The Lord is your keeper; the Lord is your shade at your right hand. 6 The sun shall not strike you by day, nor the moon by night. 7 The Lord will keep you from all evil; he will keep your life. 8 The Lord will keep your going out and your coming in from this time on and forevermore.

Before you move on, please read it aloud, slowly and prayerfully.

10. ***PERSONAL PRAYER RESPONSE.*** Nehemiah has taught us how to overcome opposition. God wants to lead us in overcoming the opposition around us. Nehemiah models how to pray and intercede to our God summarized in the acronym ABCD (starting with D):

    - **Declare** God's greatness and faithfulness with praises and Scripture,
    - **Confess** our sins and those of our nation and families,
    - **Believe** God and His Holy Word, and
    - **Ask** for what you need and use Scripture, when possible.

In the following space, please write a prayer for yourself, your family and your nation using the ABCD themes and asking for His help in opposition and the enemies you and your family face—spiritual and otherwise. Remember to spend a few minutes in silence asking God what He wants you to pray for yourself, your family or our nation. Now, prepare to intercede using the ABCD themes.

PREPARE FOR PRAYER

1) Write down your concerns.

MY CONCERNS, OPPOSITIONs, AND BROKENNESS this week INCLUDE:

2) Listen to the Holy Spirit who will guide you in prayer.

3) Recall God's greatness using scripture (see the Appendix for help with *Scriptures for Declaring God's Greatness* and *Praying with Confidence*).

4) Pray and write a summary of your prayer in the space on the next page.

MY INTERCESSORY PRAYER BASED ON NEHEMIAH 6: 1-19

- **D**eclare God's Greatness (with Scripture)

- **C**onfess the sins of your nation, your family, and yourself with the same passion as if indeed they all belonged to you.

- **B**elieve the truth of God's Word and His Faithfulness by recalling His blessings and the promises in Scripture (use those verses in prayer).

- **A**sk God for the needs He brings to mind. (Let the Holy Spirit lead you in prayer.)

8

SECURING THE GATES

Connection Question

How do you view threats to the safety of your home?

Nehemiah Gives Jobs to the People [xxxii]
St. Takla.Org
Nehemiah 7: 1-5

Chapter Eight - Securing the Gates

Attacks Abound

Last week, we joined Nehemiah and the Israelites in Jerusalem as the walls were completed. The closer they came to finishing the project, the more the opposition increased. Sanballat the Samarian, Tobiah the Ammonite, Geshem the Arab, and the "rest of the enemies" (v. 6:1) tried anything and everything to stop them. They used false calls for peace, false accusations, false prophecies—even hiring a man to speak a false prophecy, and sheer intimidation. Thanks be to God, Nehemiah through constant prayer, discernment and focus, refused the deceptions. He encouraged the people to focus on rebuilding the wall and they did. So, the walls of the city were completed in 52 days (v. 7: 15).

This week we will walk with Nehemiah as he recognizes that his building of the city wall and gates is finally completed. Now, he will begin the process of restoring the faith of his beloved people. First, however, he has to repopulate the City of Jerusalem or it would continue to be prey to many it's enemies. Although homes had been rebuilt outside the city, the inside of the city was mostly in shambles. There were large amounts of debris to be removed and protection plans to be put into place. The enemies had tried to hinder the rebuilding of the walls and gates; they would surely try to destroy the city, again so faithful people must move into Jerusalem.

Chapter Eight Questions

1. ***CONNECTION.*** In preparation for this study, please read Nehemiah 7: 1– 73 and then **circle** all the vocations or appointments mentioned. Share what you learned about Jerusalem in 444 BC from these verses.

Nehemiah 7: 1 – 73

Now when the wall had been built and I had set up the doors, and the gatekeepers, the singers, and the Levites had been appointed, 2 I gave my brother Hanani charge over Jerusalem, along with Hananiah the commander of the citadel—for he was a faithful man and feared God more than many. 3 And I said to them, "The gates of Jerusalem are not to be opened until the sun is hot; while the gatekeepers are still standing guard, let them shut and bar the doors. Appoint guards from among the inhabitants of Jerusalem, some at their watch posts, and others before their own houses." 4 The city was wide and large, but the people within it were few and no houses had been built.

5 Then my God put it into my mind to assemble the nobles and the officials and the people to be enrolled by genealogy. And I found the book of the genealogy of those who were the first to come back, and I found the following written in it:

These are the people of the province who came up out of the captivity of those exiles whom King Nebuchadnezzar of Babylon had carried into exile; they returned to Jerusalem and Judah, each to his town. 7 They came with Zerubbabel, Jeshua, Nehemiah, Azariah, Raamiah, Nahamani, Mordecai, Bilshan, Mispereth, Bigvai, Nehum, Baanah.

The number of the Israelite people: 8 the descendants of Parosh, two thousand one hundred seventy-two. 9 Of Shephatiah, three hundred seventy-two. 10 Of Arah, six hundred fifty-two. 11 Of Pahath-moab, namely the descendants of Jeshua and Joab, two thousand eight hundred eighteen. 12 Of Elam, one thousand two hundred fifty-four. 13 Of Zattu, eight hundred forty-five. 14 Of Zaccai, seven hundred sixty. 15 Of Binnui, six hundred forty-eight. 16 Of Bebai, six hundred twenty-eight. 17 Of Azgad, two thousand three hundred twenty-two. 18 Of Adonikam, six hundred sixty-seven. 19 Of Bigvai, two thousand sixty-seven. 20 Of Adin, six hundred fifty-five. 21 Of Ater, namely of Hezekiah, ninety-eight. 22 Of Hashum, three hundred twenty-eight. 2

3 Of Bezai, three hundred twenty-four. 24 Of Hariph, one hundred twelve. 25 Of Gibeon, ninety-five. 26 The people of Bethlehem and Netophah, one hundred eighty-eight. 27 Of Anathoth, one hundred twenty-eight. 28 Of Beth-azmaveth, forty-two. 29 Of Kiriath-jearim, Chephirah, and Beeroth, seven hundred forty-three. 30 Of Ramah and Geba, six hundred twenty-one. 31 Of Michmas, one hundred twenty-two. 32 Of Bethel and Ai, one hundred twenty-three. 33 Of the other Nebo, fifty-two. 34 The descendants of the other Elam, one thousand two hundred fifty-four. 35 Of Harim, three hundred twenty. 36 Of Jericho, three hundred forty-five. 37 Of Lod, Hadid, and Ono, seven hundred twenty-one. 38 Of Senaah, three thousand nine hundred thirty.

39 The priests: the descendants of Jedaiah, namely the house of Jeshua, nine hundred seventy-three. 40 Of Immer, one thousand fifty-two. 41 Of Pashhur, one thousand two hundred forty-seven. 42 Of Harim, one thousand seventeen. 43 The Levites: the descendants of Jeshua, namely of Kadmiel of the descendants of Hodevah, seventy-four. 44 The singers: the descendants of Asaph, one hundred forty-eight. 45 The gatekeepers: the descendants of Shallum, of Ater, of Talmon, of Akkub, of Hatita, of Shobai, one hundred thirty-eight. 46 The temple servants: the descendants of Ziha, of Hasupha, of Tabbaoth, 47 of Keros, of Sia, of Padon, 48 of Lebana, of Hagaba, of Shalmai, 49 of Hanan, of Giddel, of Gahar, 50 of Reaiah, of Rezin, of Nekoda, 51 of Gazzam, of Uzza, of Paseah, 52 of Besai, of Meunim, of Nephushesim, 53 of Bakbuk, of Hakupha, of Harhur, 54 of Bazlith, of Mehida, of Harsha, 55 of Barkos, of Sisera, of Temah, 56 of Neziah, of Hatipha. 57 The descendants of Solomon's servants: of Sotai, of Sophereth, of Perida, 58 of Jaala, of Darkon, of Giddel, 59 of Shephatiah, of Hattil, of Pochereth-hazzebaim, of Amon. 60 All the temple servants and the descendants of Solomon's servants were three hundred ninety-two. 61 The following were those who came up from Tel-melah, Tel-harsha, Cherub, Addon, and Immer, but they could not prove their ancestral houses or their descent, whether they belonged to Israel: 62 the descendants of Delaiah, of Tobiah, of Nekoda, six hundred forty-two. 63 Also, of the priests: the descendants of Hobaiah, of Hakkoz, of Barzillai (who had married one of the daughters of Barzillai the Gileadite and was called by their name). 64 These sought their registration among those enrolled in the genealogies, but it was not found there, so they were excluded from the priesthood as unclean; 65 the governor told them that they were not to partake of the most holy food, until a priest with Urim and Thummim* should come.

66 The whole assembly together was forty-two thousand three hundred sixty, 67 besides their male and female slaves, of whom there were seven thousand three hundred thirty-seven; and they had two hundred forty-five singers, male and female. 68 They had seven hundred thirty-six horses, two hundred forty-five mules, 69 four hundred thirty-five camels, and six thousand seven hundred twenty donkeys.

70 Now some of the heads of ancestral houses contributed to the work. The governor gave to the treasury one thousand darics of gold, fifty basins, and five hundred thirty priestly robes. 71 And some of the heads of ancestral houses gave into the building fund twenty thousand darics of gold and two thousand two hundred minas of silver. 72 And what the rest of the people gave was twenty thousand darics of gold, two thousand minas of silver, and sixty-seven priestly robes.

73 So the priests, the Levites, the gatekeepers, the singers, some of the people, the temple servants, and all Israel settled in their towns. Then the seventh month came—the people of Israel being settled in their towns—

2. ***APPOINTMENTS.*** After the walls were rebuilt and the doors put in place, what five appointments did the Governor, Nehemiah make? List them in the following space.

   i. -

   ii. -

   iii. -

   iv. -

   v. -

3. ***NEW LEADERS*** (v. 7: 1-4). Based on v. 2, how would you describe Hanani and Hananiah?

❖Ponderings

a. Why would they do a good job as leaders?

b. What three orders did Nehemiah give them (v. 3)?
    i. -

    ii. -

    iii. -

c. Why would Nehemiah order, the gates should "not be opened until the sun is hot"?

4. ***WALLS ARE UP, INHABITANTS NEEDED*** (v. 7: 1-4). What was missing in Jerusalem (v. 4)?

Fortification and Worship

The first task Nehemiah did after the walls were rebuilt and the gates put in place was to make administrative and temple appointments to fortify the city. First, he assigned gatekeepers, then singers/worshippers, and the Levites. The gatekeepers were watchmen stationed at the ten doors 24 hours per day. Later, we will read that at the temple, the gatekeepers also would be those who maintained order and reverence for the House of God (e.g., see 1 Chronicles 9: 22-29).

Nehemiah was right in first appointing the gatekeepers to watch the gates and keep the city safe from attacks, just as David and Samuel did in 1 Chronicles 9:22 (e.g., they appointed 212 to these positions of trust and responsibility to guard the house of God). Nehemiah knew that the spiritual renewal of the people was essential and watching the gates of the city to keep it free from enemies and invaders so the people could worship was vitally important.

As we have noted throughout this study, the gates have spiritual meaning for us today as does the job of gatekeeping. Gatekeepers had to be alert and watchful in everything, day and night. We too must be alert, watchful and prayerful in everything we do. Sin and temptation are always trying to knock down the gates of our minds and hearts to all kinds of evil. The enemy often nudges us to conform to the things of this culture, saying, "it isn't that bad, everyone is doing it." The Holy Spirit operating through our consciences, formed by Church teaching and the Word nudges us toward God, truth, freedom and safety. We must guard the gates to our ears, eyes, mouths, nose and emotions, where we are often exposed to temptation and then condemnation. When we refuse the gatekeeper in the Holy Spirit and in our consciences, we open ourselves to trouble and to the many tactics of the evil one who will try to pull us away from God and His ways. The Scriptures remind us to fortify ourselves and be prayerful, watchful and alert:

> **Mark 13: 33, 37.** "[Jesus] Beware, keep alert; for you do not know when the time will come. [37] And what I say to you I say to all: Keep awake."
>
> **1 Peter 5: 8.** "Discipline yourselves, keep alert. Like a roaring lion your adversary the devil prowls around, looking for someone to devour."
>
> **Ephesians 6: 13-14, 18.** "Therefore take up the whole armor of God, so that you may be able to withstand on that evil day, and having done everything, to stand firm. [14] Stand therefore, and fasten the belt of truth around your waist, and put on the breastplate of righteousness...[18] Pray in the Spirit at all times in every prayer and supplication. To that end keep alert and always persevere in supplication for all the saints."

Next, Nehemiah appointed the Levites who were the keepers of all things concerning the temple and holy items in the temple. Chronicles 6:48 points out: "their kindred, the Levites, were appointed for all the service of the tabernacle of the house of God." The Israelites would soon be celebrating the dedication of the walls and the Levites would focus on keeping all things holy.

The singers were appointed to praise the Lord day and night and to lead the worship. Nehemiah knew that the praise and worship of the Lord was the inspiration that the people needed. It also was an important part of a close relationship with God that had to be fostered and nurtured. Praise and worship to the Lord brings the power of God into the house of God and into the needs of a people. For example, in 2 Chronicles 20: 22 near the beginning of what looked like a losing battle for Judah, King Jehoshaphat appointed worshippers and singers "to sing and praise." In that, the Lord set "an ambush against the enemies"… "who had come against Judah, so that they were routed."

Worship and praise to the Lord is the way to approach the Lord. **Psalm 95: 1-2** reminds us: "O come, let us sing to the Lord; let us make a joyful noise to the rock of our salvation!
2 Let us **come into his presence** with thanksgiving; let us make a joyful noise to him with songs of praise!" Becoming a "praiser" and one who declares God's greatness in important in this life, but it is also our vocation for the next. Revelation 7: 9-12 points this out:

> "After this I looked, and there was a great multitude that no one could count, from every nation, from all tribes and peoples and languages, standing before the throne and before the Lamb, robed in white, with palm branches in their hands. 10 They cried out in a loud voice, saying, "Salvation belongs to our God who is seated on the throne, and to the Lamb!" 11 And all the angels stood around the throne and around the elders and the four living creatures, and they fell on their faces before the throne and worshiped God, 12 singing, "Amen! Blessing and glory and wisdom and thanksgiving and honor and power and might be to our God forever and ever! Amen."

5. ***THE GENEOLOGICAL RECORD*** (7: 3-5). Why did Nehemiah decide to register the people?

- Ponderings

  a. Considering all the previous opposition, why would it be important to have a record of those who returned to Jerusalem in past - with Zerubbabel, Ezra and the others?

b. List the occupations of the people.

i. (v. 39)

ii. (v. 43)

iii. (v. 44)

iv. (v. 45)

v. (v. 46)

vi. (v. 57)

Note. ***Asaph*** in v. 44 is likely a descendent of the author of Psalms 73-83 attributed to Asaph. These Psalms emphasize the themes of God's deliverance and rule over his people. They celebrate that God rescues them from foreign oppression and brings down wickedness. They remember God's saving acts on behalf of his people.

6. ***NO RECORD (7: 3-5).*** What happened to those who came, but did not have records to show their family ties (v. 61-65)?

Note. ***Urim*** **and** ***Thummim*** (signifying light and purity) were stones in a priest's breastplate that helped him to discern the will of God. The stones were used in cases where the will of God was not known and therefore, the shining of the stones would make it known. In this case, they would be used to determine if those names not recorded in the genealogies were both Jewish and Levite, and thus, could be admitted to the Holy City as priests.

The Registrants

Nehemiah Chapter 7 seems to be a turning point in the book. It turns our attention from rebuilding the wall to rebuilding the faith of the people. Nehemiah says God put it into his heart to register everyone. We see in other Scriptures registries help the people remember who their benefactors are, who their ancestors are, and who have gone before them in sacrifice, love and commitment. Historic memory is crucial to the survival of a people. It is important to God and will be the theme for the rest of the book as Nehemiah and Ezra help restore the spirit and souls of the Israelites.

The lineage of the remnant written in Chapter 7 is not the first time there was a registration of the people of God. In Genesis 35 and 46, the sons of Jacob recorded the census and journeys of the people. The Israelites to this day have always found it important to keep records of the birth, death, families, genealogies, histories, and leadership.

It seems that just as parents and grandparents love to look at the names of all their children, so does God. He loves registries and keeping a remembrance of all the names of His people and the families.[xxxiii] The Bible says he keeps those names written in "his book." For example, in Exodus, 32: 31-32 Moses was willing to have his name removed from God's book of names. He intervened for the people who "sinned a great sin" making "for themselves gods of gold" so he prayed: "If you will only forgive their sin—but if not, blot me out of the **book that you have written."**

In Daniel 12: 1, Daniel talks of a latter-day deliverance by God: "But at that time your people shall be delivered, everyone who is found **written in the book**." In Luke 10:20, Jesus even told the first 70 disciples who he sent forth to heal and preach, "Nevertheless, do not rejoice at this that the spirits submit to you."

7. ***APPLICATION.*** Nehemiah set up gatekeepers, Levites and Singers, to be watchful, to minister to his people and to worship. He wanted the people to remember who they were, who God was, and what God did for them. In application, please look back and record what you remember the Lord has done for you:

❖Ponderings

a. Do you remember the times when…

   i. He protected you from a dangerous situation -

   ii. He restored your health or gave you a healing miracle –

   iii. He put someone in your path who said something to you that Lord had for you or who had helped you in a special way deal with a difficult time –

   iv. He gave you a special miracle -

b. Do you look back on these remembrances in your prayer life when you are sad or discouraged? Do you thank the Lord for his marvelous and personal care for you? Thank Him NOW and use the space below.

8. ***PERSONAL PRAYER RESPONSE.*** In Chapter 7, Nehemiah has taught us to be watchful, prayerful and alert in our prayer lives. God wants us to become "praisers," who offer Him our thanksgivings and remember what he has done for us. Nehemiah models how to pray and intercede to our God summarized in the acronym ABCD (starting with D):

- **Declare** God's greatness and faithfulness with praises and Scripture,
- **Confess** our sins and those of our nation and families,
- **Believe** God and His Holy Word, and
- **Ask** for what you need and use Scripture, when possible.

In the following space, please write a prayer for yourself, your family and your nation using the ABCD themes and asking for the Lord's help in opposition and with the enemies you and your family face—spiritual and otherwise. Remember to spend a few minutes in silence asking God what He wants you to pray for yourself, your family or our nation. Now, prepare to intercede using the ABCD themes.

PREPARE FOR PRAYER

1) Write down your concerns.

MY CONCERNS, OPPOSITIONs, AND BROKENNESS this week INCLUDE:

2) Listen to the Holy Spirit who will guide you in prayer.

3) Recall God's greatness using scripture (see the Appendix for help with *Scriptures for Declaring God's Greatness* and *Praying with Confidence*).

4) Pray and write a summary of your prayer in the space on the next page.

MY INTERCESSORY PRAYER BASED ON NEHEMIAH CHAPTER 7

- **D**eclare God's Greatness (with Scripture)

- **C**onfess the sins of your nation, your family, and yourself with the same passion as if indeed they all belonged to you.

- **B**elieve the truth of God's Word and His Faithfulness by recalling His blessings and the promises in Scripture (use those verses in prayer).

- **A**sk God for the needs He brings to mind. (Let the Holy Spirit lead you in prayer.)

9

RESTORED

Connection Question

When you read the Scriptures, have you ever felt overwhelmed with joy or convicted of sin? Do you hunger to read the Word of God?

All the People Dwell in Booths as Moses Commanded[xxxiv]
St. Takla.Org
Nehemiah 8: 13-18

Chapter Nine - Restored

Leadership, Security and Registration

In our last study, we joined Nehemiah as he appointed leadership for the city, including the mayor, a security chief and those in charge of temple worship—this was the priority. The walls had been completed and the gates set in place. In order to safeguard the work, Nehemiah assigned "the gatekeepers, the singers [worshippers] and the Levites" (v. 7:1). The gatekeepers guarded all the doors to Jerusalem and the singers worshipped the Lord around the clock as well as led the people in praise and adoration. This praise and adoration 24/7 declares God as the Lord of Hosts [heaven's armies] who defeats the enemies and He does (e.g., see 2 Chronicles 2: 14-22).

As the governor of the region (v. 4: 14), Nehemiah appointed his brother Hanani to be in charge of Jerusalem (i.e., the mayor), and chose Hananiah to be the commander of the citadel (i.e., police chief of the inter-city fortress that included the temple and its towers). He chose Hananiah because he was "faithful" and "feared God more than many" (4: 2), meaning that he was devoted to God and His Laws and thus, would not yield to any rumors or bribes from the enemies. To further protect against enemy attacks, Nehemiah ordered the gates closed except for midday when the sun was the brightest, and the people were alert so that all could see who was coming into and leaving the city. This may remind you of Peter's words in 1 Peter 5:8, exhorting us not to sleep, but to be watchful because like a roaring lion our "adversary the devil prowls around, looking for someone to devour" or Paul words in Ephesians urging us to "stay alert," "put on the full armor of God" and "stand strong" (Ephesians 6: 1-18), "giving no place" (i.e., open gates) to the evil one (Ephesians 4: 27).

God inspired Nehemiah to register the people by family name. This was done to protect the people from those who wanted to sneak into the temple to destroy their religion and their work. Thus, the registry was based on those whose ancestry demonstrated their faithfulness and sacrifice in coming with Ezra or Zerubbabel to rebuild Jerusalem—they would be the only ones trusted to live in the city. Even in this, some may have tried to sneak into the city pretending to be priests (7: 63-64). Nehemiah ended Chapter 7 with words of satisfaction: "So the priests, the Levites, the gatekeepers, the singers, some of the people, the temple servants and all Israel settled in their towns" (v. 7: 73).

Today, Nehemiah Chapter 8 will take us to an important event that the people will celebrate in the seventh month of the Jewish calendar. We would miss its religious significance, if we did not know this seventh month celebration still appears today on Jewish calendars.

Chapter Nine Questions

1. ***RESPONDING TO THE WORD OF GOD.*** In preparation for this study, please read Nehemiah 7: 73 - 8: 18 and **circle** all the ways the people responded to hearing the Word of God. Share what you learn from their response.

Nehemiah 7: 73 - 8: 18

73 So the priests, the Levites, the gatekeepers, the singers, some of the people, the
temple servants, and all Israel settled in their towns. When the **seventh month** came—
the people of Israel being settled in their towns—8: 1 all the people gathered together
into the square before the Water Gate. They told the scribe Ezra to bring the book of
the Law of Moses, which the Lord had given to Israel. 2 Accordingly, the priest Ezra
brought the law before the assembly, both men and women and all who could hear
with understanding. This was on the first day of the seventh month.

3 He read from it facing the square before the Water Gate from early morning until midday, in the presence of the men and the women and those who could understand; and the ears of all the people were attentive to the book of the law. 4 The scribe Ezra stood on a wooden platform that had been made for the purpose; and beside him stood Mattithiah, Shema, Anaiah, Uriah, Hilkiah, and Maaseiah on his right hand; and Pedaiah, Mishael, Malchijah, Hashum, Hash-baddanah, Zechariah, and Meshullam on his left hand.

Ezra's Prayer to God

And Ezra opened the book in the sight of all the people, for he was standing above all the people; and when he opened it, all the people stood up. 6 Then Ezra blessed the Lord, the great God, and all the people answered, "Amen, Amen," lifting up their hands. Then they bowed their heads and worshiped the Lord with their faces to the ground. 7 Also Jeshua, Bani, Sherebiah, Jamin, Akkub, Shabbethai, Hodiah, Maaseiah, Kelita, Azariah, Jozabad, Hanan, Pelaiah, the Levites, helped the people to understand the law, while the people remained in their places. 8 So they read from the book, from the law of God, with interpretation. They gave the sense, so that the people understood the reading.

9 And Nehemiah, who was the governor, and Ezra the priest and scribe, and the Levites who taught the people said to all the people, "This day is holy to the Lord your God; do not mourn or weep." For all the people wept when they heard the words of the law. 10 Then he said to them, "Go your way, eat the fat and drink sweet wine and send portions of them to those for whom nothing is prepared, for this day is holy to our Lord; and do not be grieved, for the joy of the Lord is your strength." 11 So the Levites stilled all the people, saying, "Be quiet, for this day is holy; do not be grieved." 12 And all the people went their way to eat and drink and to send portions and to make great rejoicing, because they had understood the words that were declared to them.

13 On the second day the heads of ancestral houses of all the people, with the priests and the Levites, came together to the scribe Ezra in order to study the words of the law. 14 And they found it written in the law, which the Lord had commanded by Moses, that the people of Israel should live in booths during the festival of the seventh month, 15 and that they should publish and proclaim in all their towns and in Jerusalem as follows, "Go out to the hills and bring branches of olive, wild olive, myrtle, palm, and other leafy trees to make booths, as it is written."

16 So the people went out and brought them, and made booths for themselves, each on
the roofs of their houses, and in their courts and in the courts of the house of God, and
in the square at the Water Gate and in the square at the Gate of Ephraim. 17 And all the
assembly of those who had returned from the captivity made booths and lived in
them; for from the days of Jeshua son of Nun to that day the people of Israel had not
done so. And there was very great rejoicing. 18 And day-by-day, from the first day to
the last day, he read from the book of the law of God. They kept the festival seven
days; and on the eighth day there was a solemn assembly, according to the ordinance.
NRSVCE

2. ***THE GATHERING*** (v. 1-2). Who gathered together and what was the purpose of the gathering?

❖Ponderings

a. At what time of year did the people gather (v. 1)?

b. Where did they gather (v.1)?

New Year's Day

In October 444 B.C., the New Year's Day of the Hebrew "civil" calendar, the people were celebrating *Rosh Hashanah* (which in Hebrew means the head or beginning of the new year) as well as the Biblical festival called the *Feast of Trumpets*. We know this because the Lord said to Moses in **Leviticus 23: 23-24**:

> "Speak to the people of Israel, saying: In the seventh month, on the first day of the month, you shall observe a day of complete rest, a holy convocation commemorated with trumpet blasts. [25] You shall not work at your occupations; and you shall present the Lord's offering by fire."

In Israel, trumpets were blown on the first day of every month of the year. **Psalm 81:** 3, tells us that God commanded the Israelites to: "Blow the trumpet at the new moon, at the full moon, on our festal day." Thus, the blowing of trumpets had great meaning for the people: 1) to announce the first day of the month or important feast days, 2) to call the people to assemble, or 3) to mobilize the army. In this case, the sound of the trumpet meant both the first day of the month and a religious feast day. The Hebrews had two calendars, a civil one to mark the beginning and ending of the agricultural seasons, and a liturgical one. We will discover more about the religious calendar feasts in the next chapter.

3. ***EZRA*** (v. 1-2). Who was Ezra (v. 1-2)?

❖Ponderings

a. Read Ezra 7: 1-5 and record what you further learn about Ezra and his heritage.

Ezra 7: 1-5. After this, in the reign of King Artaxerxes of Persia, Ezra son of Seraiah, son of Azariah, son of Hilkiah, 2 son of Shallum, son of Zadok, son of Ahitub, 3 son of Amariah, son of Azariah, son of Meraioth, 4 son of Zerahiah, son of Uzzi, son of Bukki, 5 son of Abishua, son of Phinehas, son of Eleazar, son of the chief priest Aaron— 6 this Ezra went up from Babylonia. He was a scribe* skilled in the law of Moses that the Lord the God of Israel had given; and the king granted him all that he asked, for the hand of the Lord his God was upon him. 7 Some of the people of Israel, and some of the priests and Levites, the singers and gatekeepers, and the temple servants also went up to Jerusalem, in the seventh year of King Artaxerxes.

Note. Scribes were teachers, who often served as secretaries (e.g., in Jeremiah 36:32, where Baruch wrote down what the prophet Jeremiah spoke). Later they became known as scholars who studied God's laws and could teach the Scriptures to others. At the time of Jesus, the scribes were priests and members of the Pharisees.

b. What did Ezra bring to the people (Nehemiah 8: 1)?

c. Who came to listen?

4. ***THE PUBLIC SQUARE*** (v. 3-9). Describe the scene in the public square located near the Water Gate in v. 3-9.

   a. The Reader (v. 3-4) – Who, where and what?

   b. The Duration (v. 3) – The time period?

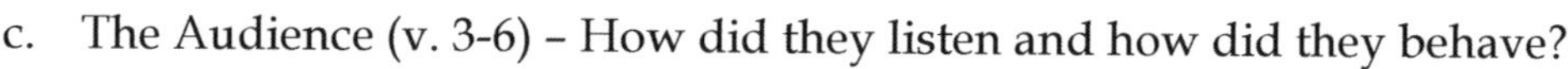

   c. The Audience (v. 3-6) – How did they listen and how did they behave?

   d. The Prayer and Worship (v. 6) – How did the people respond to God's Word?

   e. The Levites (v. 7-8) – What part did they play?

5. ***WEEPING*** (v. 9). When the people heard the message, how did the respond?

❖Ponderings

   a. What do you think they mourned?

   b. Why do you think they wept?

6. ***BE QUIET*** (v. 9-11). Describe who calmed the people and what they said.

   a. Nehemiah and Ezra (v. 9-10) said:

   b. The Levites (v. 11) said:

7. ***THE JOY OF THE LORD IS YOUR STRENGTH*** (v. 10-12). What brought joy to the people?

   ❖Ponderings

   a. What is the Joy of the Lord and how is it your/our strength?

   b. How is the Word of God related to joy?

   c. How is grieving over sin, returning to God and receiving forgiveness connected to real joy?

   d. What can the Word of God do to transform our thinking so that we no longer have to rely on the world, the media, the workplace or the enemies of God to tell us what to believe or think?

Hunger for God's Word

In this chapter, we joined all the Israelites who came together at the City Square near the Water Gate. It was the first day of the seventh month and some may have remembered it was the Feast of Trumpets, which they had given up celebrating in their brokenness, during the captivity and other devastations. Ezra brought the "Law of Moses, which the Lord had given to Israel (v. 1) and stood on a wooden platform. When he opened the book, likely the first five books of the Bible—Genesis, Exodus, Leviticus, Numbers and Deuteronomy—the people stood up. He read the Word of the Lord from morning to midday (v. 1-5). Obviously, the people were starved and thirsty for the Word of God and they stayed focused because they knew how uninformed and desperate they were, needing God's help in everything. It takes only a few fallen-away generations to leave the next ones destitute and ignorant about the things and ways of God. Then Ezra blessed the Lord, the great God. All the people responded, "Amen, Amen" and lifted up their hands as a sign of fervent agreement and prayer. They bowed and worshiped the Lord with their faces to the ground as a sign of complete submission and adoration. Then the Levites walked among them helping them understand what was read.

When the people heard and understood the Word of God, they began to mourn and weep. This is what beholding his Word and His splendor do in our lives—we more clearly see the evil, the sin and all that is wrong with our lives, our families and our nation. In this case, Governor Nehemiah and Priest Ezra responded, "This day is holy to the Lord your God; do not mourn or weep" (v. 9). They told them to celebrate the feast day: "Go your way, eat the fat and drink sweet wine and send portions of them to those for whom nothing is prepared, for this day is holy to our Lord; and do not be grieved, **for the joy of the Lord is your strength**." Then the Levites quieted the people, saying, "Be quiet, for this day is holy; do not be grieved" (v. 11). "And all the people went their way to eat and drink and to send portions and to make great rejoicing, because they had understood the words that were declared to them."

It took hearing and understanding the Word of God to begin healing broken hearts and dreams. The Word of God had revealed the sin in their lives and they were grieved. Confessing their sins brought God's forgiveness. It is only God who can change lives and hearts and nations. It is only God who can comfort the mourning of disobedience and the consequences of sin. Here in Jerusalem, we see His comfort and the great JOY brought to the people. The words of **Psalm 107: 19-20** came to pass and they can still guide us today: "Then they cried to the Lord in their trouble, and he saved them from their distress; he sent out his word and healed them."

8. ***THE FEAST OF BOOTHS*** (v. 13-15). What did the people discover when they read the "Law commanded by Moses" (i.e., the Word of God) concerning a feast in the seventh month?

❖Ponderings

a. Read Leviticus 23: 39-44 and further explain what was the purpose of building "the booths"?

Leviticus 23:39-44. "On the fifteenth day of the seventh month, when you
have gathered in the produce of the land, you shall keep the feast of the
Lord seven days; on the first day shall be a solemn rest, and on the eighth
day shall be a solemn rest. 40 And you shall take on the first day the fruit of
goodly trees, branches of palm trees, and boughs of leafy trees, and
willows of the brook; and you shall rejoice before the Lord your God
seven days. 41 You shall keep it as a feast to the Lord seven days in the
year; it is a statute forever throughout your generations; you shall keep it
in the seventh month. 42 You shall dwell in booths for seven days; all that
are native in Israel shall dwell in booths, 43 that your generations may
know that I made the people of Israel dwell in booths when I brought
them out of the land of Egypt: I am the Lord your God." 44 Thus Moses
declared to the people of Israel the appointed feasts of the Lord.

b. What could the "feast of booths" symbolize for you today?

c. Do you have a booth in your home where you can meet the Lord?

The Feast of Booths

The *Feast of Booths,* also called *Feast of Tabernacles* (or Sukkot in Hebrew), is still celebrated from the 15th to the 22nd of the seventh month, called Tishri (late September to early October on our calendars). It was God's desire that the Israelites remember and commemorate how He called them out of slavery in Egypt and cared for them. He wanted them to remember how he delivered them from the armies of Egypt by parting the Red Sea and giving them a passage onto dry ground, allowing the waters to close over all their pursuing armies. He wanted them to recall how they wandered in the desert for 40 years, living in booths or huts, while God provided for them. They grumbled persistently and even worshipped a golden calf, but God in His great love provided heavenly manna for food and guided them into the Promised Land. The Feast of Booths commemorates God's provision and guidance, and the Israelites must live in huts to celebrate it.[xxxv] By celebrating this feast, the people were recommitting themselves to follow God in everything.

God commanded the Israelites to celebrate the Feast that He established since the time of Joshua. The priests had to offer many blood sacrifices for the sins of the people while the people individually repented and worshipped in booths or tents (made as they would have lived in the dessert). Thus, when we joined the people in Nehemiah 8, we note they had two weeks to prepare for the feast as they were reading God's Word on the second day of the seventh month (Nehemiah 8: 2). Even though God called the Israelites to yearly celebrate the Feast of Booths, the people of God had not always obeyed. They sinned against God in so many ways. After much suffering for their lack of obedience and sin, the exiles in Jerusalem in 444 BC repented and set their minds and hearts to obey God's commandments and His Word. While the priests offered the sacrifices for sin, the people rejoiced in God's presence. They celebrated His forgiveness, His protection, His deliverance, and His provisions. It was God's Word that led them to repent and confess their sins. God's Word changed everything for them, and it will do the same for us today. It called them to worship and as they turned around to obey His Word, they were filled with much joy.

What could the Feast of Booths mean to us today? **Hebrews 12: 18-28** reminds us that Jesus, is our sacrifice for sin and our celebration, and we need to worship Him and be thankful:

"You have not come to something that can be touched, a blazing fire, and darkness, and gloom, and a tempest, [19] and the sound of a trumpet, … [22] But you have come to Mount Zion and to the city of the living God, the heavenly Jerusalem, and to innumerable angels in festal gathering, [23] and to the assembly of the firstborn who are enrolled in heaven, and to God the judge of all, and to the spirits of the righteous made perfect, [24] and to Jesus, the mediator of a new covenant, and to the sprinkled blood that speaks a better word than the blood of Abel. [25] See that you do not refuse the one who is speaking; for if they did not escape when they refused the one who warned them on earth, how much less will we escape if we reject the one who warns from heaven! … [28] therefore, since we are receiving a kingdom that cannot be shaken, let us give thanks, by which we offer to God an acceptable worship with reverence and awe; [29] for indeed our God is a consuming fire."

In **John 1: 14**, we read that: "the Word became flesh and ***dwelt*** among us, full of grace and truth; we have beheld his glory, glory as of the only Son from the Father." The word translated ***dwelt*** from New Testament Greek is "eskēnōsen," which means more accurately **tabernacled, tented or sojourned** with us. In **John 7: 37-39**, Jesus tells us that HE lives with us always because the Holy Spirit lives in us. Now that is something to celebrate always:

"On the last day of the festival, the great day, while Jesus was standing there, he cried out, 'Let anyone who is thirsty come to me, [38] and let the one who believes in me drink. As the scripture has said, 'Out of the believer's heart shall flow rivers of living water.' [39] Now he said this about the Spirit, which believers in him were to receive; for as yet there was no Spirit, because Jesus was not yet glorified.'"

9. ***APPLICATION.*** The people were starved to hear the Word of God. When they did, they wept over their sin and rejoiced over God's ways—His forgiveness and love. They celebrated the feast day that He had established. Now is a good time to consider how each one of us respects and honors the Word of God:

   a. **Listen.** How often do you listen for God to speak to you in His Holy Word—are the Scriptures alive and active in your life (Hebrew 4: 12)?

   b. **Discern.** According to Romans 12: 1-2, how can you discern God's will/ways and how does that relate to what happened to the Israelites as they heard the Word of the Lord?

Romans 12: 1-2. I appeal to you therefore, brothers and sisters, by the mercies of God, to present your bodies as a living sacrifice, holy and acceptable to God, which is your spiritual worship. 2 Do not be conformed to this world, but be transformed by the renewing of your minds, so that you may discern what is the will of God—what is good and acceptable and perfect.

   c. **The Joy of the Lord.** How can you make the joy of the Lord your strength?

   d. **Delight.** What meaning does Psalm 1: 1-3 add to finding the *Joy of the Lord* in our lives?

Psalm 1: 1-3. Happy are those who do not follow the advice of the wicked, or take the path that sinners tread, or sit in the seat of scoffers; 2 but their delight is in the law of the Lord, and on his law, they meditate day and night. 3 They are like trees planted by streams of water, which yield their fruit in its season, and their leaves do not wither. In all that they do, they prosper.

   e. **Your Booth.** Write down a place in your home that can be your booth for praise, prayerful remembrance, and thanksgiving. Then plan to set aside time to rejoice in the Lord, and to remember what He has done for you, with thanksgivings and reading and pondering His Holy Word.

10. ***PERSONAL PRAYER RESPONSE.*** Nehemiah has taught us much about joy, the importance of the Word of God, thanksgiving, prayer, praise and faith. God wants to fill us with the Joy of the Holy Spirit (Galatians 5). Nehemiah models how to pray to our **Awesome** God using the acronym ABCD (starting with D):

- Declare God's greatness and faithfulness with praises and Scripture,
- Confess our sins and those of our nation and families,
- Believe God and His Holy Word, and
- Ask for what you need and use Scripture, when possible.

In the following space, please write a prayer for yourself, your family and your nation using the ABCD themes and the verses from our study of Nehemiah 8, Romans 12: 1-2, and Psalm 1: 1-3, especially related to listening to the Scriptures, receiving forgiveness and rejoicing. Psalm 119: 110-111 says to us: Your decrees are my heritage forever; they are the joy of my heart. I incline my heart to perform your statutes forever, to the end.

Remember to spend a few minutes in silence asking God what He wants you to pray for yourself, your family or our nation. Now, prepare to intercede using the ABCD themes.

PREPARE FOR PRAYER

1) Write down your concerns.

MY CONCERNS AND/OR OPEN GATES WHERE I NEED JOY INCLUDE:

2) Listen to the Holy Spirit who will guide you in prayer.

3) Recall God's greatness using scripture (see the Appendix for help with *Scriptures for Declaring God's Greatness* and *Praying with Confidence*).

4) Pray and write a summary of your prayer in the space on the next page.

MY INTERCESSORY PRAYER BASED ON NEHEMIAH 7: 73 8: 18

- **D**eclare God's Greatness (with Scripture)

- **C**onfess the sins of your nation, your family, and yourself with the same passion as if indeed they all belonged to you.

- **B**elieve the truth of God's Word and His Faithfulness by recalling His blessings and the promises in Scripture (use those verses in prayer).

- **A**sk God for the needs He brings to mind. (Let the Holy Spirit lead you in prayer.)

10

NATIONAL CONFESSION

Connection Question

What does CONFESSION mean to you today? Do you confess your sins daily to the Lord and participate regularly in the sacrament of reconciliation?

All the People Wept[xxxvi]
"All the people wept, when they heard the words of the Law of God"
St. Takla.Org
Nehemiah 8:9

Chapter Ten - National Confession

Celebrating God's Goodness

In our last study, we joined all the Israelites who came together on the first day of the seventh month, called Rosh Hashanah and the Feast of Trumpets. In their sin and brokenness, they had given up celebrating the God-ordained feast days, but now it was time to rededicate their lives to God.

The Priest Ezra brought the "Law of Moses, which the Lord had given to Israel," including the first five books of the Bible—Genesis, Exodus, Leviticus, Numbers and Deuteronomy. All the people stood up as Ezra read the Word of the Lord from morning to midday (v. 1-5). The people knew they were starved for the Word of God and they stayed focused for many hours. They also knew they needed God's guidance and help in everything. Then Ezra blessed "the Lord, the great God" and all the people said, "Amen, Amen" and lifted up their hands as a sign of fervent agreement, praise and worship. They bowed with their faces to the ground indicating complete submission and adoration to the Lord.

As they heard more of the Word of God, the people fell on their faces with weeping and repentance for their sins—they knew they had fallen from God's laws. Nehemiah and Ezra told the people to remember what the Lord had done for them—He delivered them from slavery by parting the Red Sea and then fed them manna from heaven in the desert for 40 years. Nehemiah exhorted the people to continue to celebrate for the "**joy of the Lord was their strength**."

Immediately, the people made plans to celebrate the *Feast of Booth* (also translated the *Feast of Tabernacles* or *Sukkot* in Hebrew), which the Lord had commanded This meant the heads of each family would build booths (i.e., huts) and then the family would spend seven days in them remembering God's goodness with thanksgiving before Him. This Feast was God's desire for the Israelites to commemorate how He called them out of slavery in Egypt and he cared for them. He wanted them to remember how he delivered them from the armies of Egypt by parting the Red Sea and giving them a passage onto dry ground but allowing the waters to close over all the pursuing armies. He wanted them to recall how they wondered in the desert for 40 years, living in booths or huts. They grumbled persistently and even worshipped a golden calf, but God in His great love provided heavenly manna and guided them into the Promised Land. Thus the Feast of Booths was to be celebrated yearly to commemorate God's provision and guidance and the Israelites must live in huts to celebrate it.

Today, we join the people in Nehemiah 9, following their celebration of the Feast of Booths (after many years of neglecting God's Word by not celebrating the great feast). Now with a new focus on the Word of God and obedience, they gather together with weeping and fasting for a time of national confession of their sins.

Chapter Ten Questions

1. ***NATIONAL CONFESSION.*** In preparation for this study, please read Nehemiah 9: 1 – 37 and **circle** the ideas (under each of the labels) that get your attention. Share why these ideas or verses caught your attention.

Nehemiah 9: 1 - 38

Now on the twenty-fourth day of this month the people of Israel were assembled with
fasting and in sackcloth, and with earth* on their heads. 2 Then those of Israelite descent
separated themselves from all foreigners, and stood and confessed their sins and the
iniquities of their ancestors. 3 They stood up in their place and read from the book of the
law of the Lord their God for a fourth part of the day, and for another fourth they made
confession and worshiped the Lord their God. 4 Then Jeshua, Bani, Kadmiel, Shebaniah,
Bunni, Sherebiah, Bani, and Chenani stood on the stairs of the Levites and cried out with a
loud voice to the Lord their God.

5Then the Levites, Jeshua, Kadmiel, Bani, Hashabneiah, Sherebiah, Hodiah, Shebaniah,
and Pethahiah, said, "Stand up and bless the Lord your God from everlasting to
everlasting. Blessed be your glorious name, which is exalted above all blessing and
praise." 6 And Ezra said: "You are the Lord, you alone; you have made heaven, the heaven
of heavens, with all their host, the earth and all that is on it, the seas and all that is in them.
To all of them you give life, and the host of heaven worships you. 7 You are the Lord, the
God who chose Abram and brought him out of Ur of the Chaldeans and gave him the
name Abraham; 8 and you found his heart faithful before you, and made with him a
covenant to give to his descendants the land of the Canaanite, the Hittite, the Amorite, the
Perizzite, the Jebusite, and the Girgashite; and you have fulfilled your promise, for you are
righteous.

9 "And you saw the distress of our ancestors in Egypt and heard their cry at the Red Sea. 10
You performed signs and wonders against Pharaoh and all his servants and all the people
of his land, for you knew that they acted insolently against our ancestors. You made a
name for yourself, which remains to this day. 11 And you divided the sea before them, so
that they passed through the sea on dry land, but you threw their pursuers into the
depths, like a stone into mighty waters.

12 Moreover, you led them by day with a pillar of cloud, and by night with a pillar of fire,
to give them light on the way in which they should go. 13 You came down also upon
Mount Sinai, and spoke with them from heaven, and gave them right ordinances and true
laws, good statutes and commandments, 14 and you made known your holy Sabbath to
them and gave them commandments and statutes and a law through your servant Moses.
15 For their hunger you gave them bread from heaven, and for their thirst you brought
water for them out of the rock, and you told them to go in to possess the land that you
swore to give them.

16 "But they and our ancestors acted presumptuously and stiffened their necks and did not
obey your commandments; 17 they refused to obey, and were not mindful of the wonders
that you performed among them; but they stiffened their necks and determined to return
to their slavery in Egypt. But you are a God ready to forgive, gracious and merciful, slow
to anger and abounding in steadfast love, and you did not forsake them.

18 Even when they had cast an image of a calf for themselves and said, 'This is your God
who brought you up out of Egypt,' and had committed great blasphemies, 19 you in your
great mercies did not forsake them in the wilderness; the pillar of cloud that led them in
the way did not leave them by day, nor the pillar of fire by night that gave them light on
the way by which they should go. 20 You gave your good spirit to instruct them, and did
not withhold your manna from their mouths, and gave them water for their thirst. 21 Forty
years you sustained them in the wilderness so that they lacked nothing; their clothes did
not wear out and their feet did not swell. 22 And you gave them kingdoms and peoples,
and allotted to them every corner, so they took possession of the land of King Sihon of
Heshbon and the land of King Og of Bashan. 23 You multiplied their descendants like the
stars of heaven, and brought them into the land that you had told their ancestors to enter
and possess. 24 So the descendants went in and possessed the land, and you subdued
before them the inhabitants of the land, the Canaanites, and gave them into their hands,
with their kings and the peoples of the land, to do with them as they pleased. 25 And they
captured fortress cities and a rich land, and took possession of houses filled with all sorts
of goods, hewn cisterns, vineyards, olive orchards, and fruit trees in abundance; so they
ate, and were filled and became fat, and delighted themselves in your great goodness.

26 "Nevertheless they were disobedient and rebelled against you and cast your law behind
their backs and killed your prophets, who had warned them in order to turn them back to
you, and they committed great blasphemies. 27 Therefore you gave them into the hands of
their enemies, who made them suffer. Then in the time of their suffering they cried out to
you and you heard them from heaven, and according to your great mercies you gave them
saviors who saved them from the hands of their enemies. 28 But after they had rest, they
again did evil before you, and you abandoned them to the hands of their enemies, so that
they had dominion over them; yet when they turned and cried to you, you heard from
heaven, and many times you rescued them according to your mercies. 29

And you warned them in order to turn them back to your law. Yet they acted
presumptuously and did not obey your commandments, but sinned against your
ordinances, by the observance of which a person shall live. They turned a stubborn
shoulder and stiffened their neck and would not obey. 30 Many years you were patient
with them, and warned them by your spirit through your prophets; yet they would not
listen. Therefore, you handed them over to the peoples of the lands. 31 Nevertheless, in
your great mercies you did not make an end of them or forsake them, for you are a
gracious and merciful God.

32 "Now therefore, our God—the great and mighty and awesome God, keeping covenant
and steadfast love—do not treat lightly all the hardship that has come upon us, upon our
kings, our officials, our priests, our prophets, our ancestors, and all your people, since the
time of the kings of Assyria until today. 33 You have been just in all that has come upon us,
for you have dealt faithfully and we have acted wickedly; 34 our kings, our officials, our
priests, and our ancestors have not kept your law or heeded the commandments and the
warnings that you gave them. 35 Even in their own kingdom, and in the great goodness
you bestowed on them, and in the large and rich land that you set before them, they did
not serve you and did not turn from their wicked works. 36 Here we are, slaves to this
day—slaves in the land that you gave to our ancestors to enjoy its fruit and its good gifts.
37 Its rich yield goes to the kings whom you have set over us because of our sins; they have
power also over our bodies and over our livestock at their pleasure, and we are in great
distress."

The Signing of the Covenant

38 Because of all this we make a firm agreement in writing, and on that sealed document
are inscribed the names of our officials, our Levites, and our priests." NRSVCE

Note. "With earth on their heads" (v.2) refers to an Old Testament practice of putting dirt or ashes on the head to show repentance, humility toward God, and turning away from sins.

2. ***CONFESSION SIN*** (9: 1-5). What was the occasion for the gathering and the timing in the schedule (how was the day spent) (v. 1)?

❖Ponderings

a. Why would the Israelites repent of sins for their ancestors (v. 2)?

b. What were the elements in their time of confession (v. 3-5)?

National Day of Confession

The Israelites read from the Book of the Law - the Pentateuch that reminded them of how far they had turned away from God. They were brokenhearted when they heard God's Word, so they confessed their sins and proclaimed God's greatness and faithfulness. They did this in the midst of challenging and difficult circumstances, including having to rebuild their own homes amid rubbish, facing never-ending antagonistic attacks from surrounding enemies, and living in severe poverty while watching their children become enslaved (v. 37-38). They had separated themselves from foreigners so they could stand before God to represent the many sins of their fathers, who had fallen away from God's commandments.

The people were in great distress and knowing it was caused by the sinfulness passed on from previous generations as well as the evil in their own hearts. They realized they were helpless without God. They knew they had to repent and ask God's forgiveness to start anew as a nation committed to following the Lord so they fasted, wept and "confessed their sins and the iniquities of their ancestors…and worshiped the Lord their God" (v. 3). In three hours of confession, and three hours of worship and praise (v. 3), they humbly presented themselves to God as dependent on Him in everything. The Levites encouraged them saying, "Stand up and bless the Lord your God from everlasting to everlasting. Blessed be your glorious name, which is exalted above all blessing and praise."

3. ***PRAISING GOD'S FAITHFULNESS*** (V. 5-28). Fill in the following chart to summarize 1) what God had done in His power and 2) the praises the Israelites expressed to God.

Nehemiah 9 Verses	PRAISES to GOD - His GREATNESS and POWER
5-6	Example: Creator— of the earth, the seas, giver life of everything - heavenly host worships.
7-8	Abraham—
9-12	Deliverance out of Egypt—
13-15	The Law and Food—
16-18	Forgiveness—
19-21	Provision—
22-25	Goodness—
26-27	Great compassion—
28	Deliverance—

4. ***GOD'S MERCY*** (9: 25-28). In the cycle of the Israelite's rebellion, there would be a cry for God's faithfulness and a return to God, and then a falling into sin again. In all this, God would show his love and faithfulness. List Israel's sins and rebellion, their cry to God and God's faithfulness from Nehemiah 9: 25-28 using the chart below.

Israel's Cycle of Sin		
Israel's Sin and Rebellion	Israel's Cry to God	God's Faithfulness
v. 23-25		
V. 27		
V. 28		

5. ***THE NEED*** (V. 36-38). What need are the people bringing before God in v. 36-38?

❖Ponderings

   a. What did the Israelites do in Nehemiah 9: 28-38 prior to making a request to God?

   b. What can we depend on NOW on when we come to God, and what can we offer God prior to making a request? See Hebrews 10: 19-25 and 13: 15.

Hebrews 10: 12-25. Therefore, brethren, since we have confidence to enter the sanctuary by the blood of Jesus, [20] by the new and living way which he opened for us through the curtain, that is, through his flesh, [21] and since we have a great priest over the house of God, [22] let us draw near with a true heart in full assurance of faith, with our hearts sprinkled clean from an evil conscience and our bodies washed with pure water. [23] Let us hold fast the confession of our hope without wavering, for he who promised is faithful; [24] and let us consider how to stir up one another to love and good works, [25] not neglecting to meet together, as is the habit of some, but encouraging one another, and all the more as you see the Day drawing near.

Hebrews 13: 15-16. Through him, then, let us continually offer a sacrifice of praise to God, that is, the fruit of lips that confess his name.

Broken Hearts Over Sin Lead to Revival in the Nation

The more the Israelites read God's Word, the more they realized how faithful God had been to them, even in their disobedience. They praised God for all His providential care, for His many signs and wonders on their behalf as a nation. The cried out in sorrow for having "stiffened their necks "and "not obeying the commandments." They had not kept God in mind, but instead "stiffened their necks" and "determined to return to slavery in Egypt." They praised God for not forsaking them when they "cast an image of a calf" and "committed great blasphemies." They praised God for his mercies of continuing to guide them in the wilderness with a "pillar of cloud by day" and a "pillar of fire by night." They praised Him for sustaining them with water and manna for 40 years during which time "their clothes did not wear out and their feet did not swell." They praised God for bringing them into the promised land of "vineyards, olive orchards, and fruit trees in abundance" so that they ate and "became fat and delighted themselves" in God's "great goodness."

Even after experiencing such great faithfulness of God, the next generation "rebels against God," casts his "law behind their backs" and "killed the prophets who warned them to turn back" from their blasphemies. Thus, the Israelites again begin what might be called the *rebellion-revival* cycle, including: 1) They rebel, turn from God to sin, idolatry and wickedness -> 2) After prophetic warnings, they fall into hands of their enemies -> 3) They cry out to God from oppression; they recall His faithfulness and they repent -> 4) God intervenes and rescues them and they return to Him in everything enjoying God's blessings, -> but eventually they rebel again, fall away into sin and wickedness, and the cycle begins again.

At this juncture in praising God for His greatness and faithfulness, they begin to repent of their own unfaithfulness, transgression of His commandments, and neglect of warnings from God. They know they are "slaves to this day" because of their sins. They are ready to make a new covenant with God, so they call upon the merciful covenant-making God with "an agreement in writing" to follow Him again in everything (v. 38).

6. ***THE REBELLION-REVIVAL CYCLE*** <u>(V. 36-38).</u> What did you learn about the *rebellion-revival cycle* as presented in this chapter (see the summary chart below)? What parts could apply to our nation, our families or our lives today?

THE FOUR-STAGE REBELLION-REVIVAL CYCLE
i. **Rebellion.** They rebel against God to turn to evil, making Gods of many things.
ii. **Warnings and Consequences.** After numerous warnings from God through the prophets and teachers, they fall into the hands of their enemies.
iii. **Repentance.** They cry out to God from oppression, remembering His faithfulness and realizing their sinfulness and spiritual depravity.
iv. **Intervention.** God intervenes and rescues them from their oppressors. They repent and return to following God in everything and enjoying His blessings.
Rebellion again. They turn away from God. God sends warnings, which go unheeded. They fall into the hands of their enemies and the cycle begins AGAIN.

7. ***APPLICATION.*** When Nehemiah was sent to rebuild the physical walls and gates, he was also rebuilding spiritual gates and walls of faith. Please ask God where the broken or open gates are in your life, your family, our nation—spiritual or otherwise— and what you can learn from Nehemiah that will help you rebuild them. Consider the following application questions:

   a. How will you stop the *rebellion-revival* cycle in yourself, your family or your nation?

   b. When you want to be renewed in your spiritual life, God through the Book of Nehemiah shows us where to begin: confession of sin, adoration and praises to the glorious God of all the heavens and the earth. With that in mind, what can you do to start revival, meaning a recovery of an on fire" spiritual life, in this nation and in your life and that of your family?

   c. True repentance always means a change in direction. In Nehemiah 9:38, the people promised God a change in direction. What change is God calling you to make in your life at this time?

   d. When great change and revival is needed in your life and in those around you, God through the Book of Nehemiah shows how essential it is to hear, read, and take the Word of God to heart and mind. What can you do beginning with the reading and praying with the *Word of God* to start a revival in your life or in those around you?

e. Prayer is the only answer to the changes needed in our lives, our families and our nation. How will you change your prayer life? How can you unite with other "pray-ers" to cry out to the Lord for help and change?

8. ***PERSONAL PRAYER RESPONSE.*** Please write a prayer using any of the verses or related Scriptures from our study of Nehemiah 9, especially related to confession of personal, family and national sins, adoration or praising the Lord, increasing your prayer time, rebuilding broken gates or what you can do to bring a new revival of faith and repentance to those around you. Nehemiah models how to pray and intercede to our **Awesome** God summarized in the acronym ABCD (starting with D):

   - **Declare** God's greatness and faithfulness with praises and Scripture,
   - **Confess** our sins and those of our nation and families,
   - **Believe** God and His Holy Word, and
   - **Ask** for what you need and use Scripture, when possible.

   In the space below, please write a prayer for yourself, your family and your nation using the ABCD themes and the verses from our study of Nehemiah 9. Remember to spend a few minutes in silence asking God what He wants you to pray for yourself, your family or our nation. Now, prepare to intercede using the ABCD themes.

PREPARE FOR PRAYER

1) Write down your concerns.

MY CONCERNS, OPEN GATES OR BROKEN WALLS INCLUDE:

2) Listen to the Holy Spirit who will guide you in prayer.

3) Recall God's greatness using scripture (see the Appendix for help with *Scriptures for Declaring God's Greatness* and *Praying with Confidence*).

4) Pray and write a summary of your prayer in the space on the next page.

MY INTERCESSORY PRAYER BASED ON NEHEMIAH 9

- **D**eclare God's Greatness (with Scripture)

- **C**onfess the sins of your nation, your family, and yourself with the same passion as if indeed they all belonged to you.

- **B**elieve the truth of God's Word and His Faithfulness by recalling His blessings and the promises in Scripture (use those verses in prayer).

- **A**sk God for the needs He brings to mind. (Let the Holy Spirit lead you in prayer.)

11

MOVING TO JERUSALEM

Connection Question

What does it mean to you when you sign your name to a legal document?

The People Listen to the Book of the Law xxxvii
They Pledge to Be Faithful
St.Takla.Org
Nehemiah 9: 1- 10: 37

Chapter Eleven – Moving to Jerusalem

Remembering and Praising

In our last study, we joined the Israelites as Ezra read God's Word to them and they realized how disobedient they had been to God. Their families and ancestors had fallen into what could be called a *rebellion-revival cycle:*

- **Rebellion.** In spite of God's great faithfulness and care, each generation REBELLS against God and His law.

- **Warnings and Consequences.** After WARNING them continually through the prophets and teachers, but to no avail, God allows them to fall into the hands of their enemies.

- **Repentance.** Before long, they cry out to God from their oppression and enslavement. They become aware of their gross sinfulness and spiritual depravity. They recall God's faithfulness and mighty works. They REPENT.

- **Intervention.** God INTERVENES and rescues them from the enemy oppressors. The people REVIVE their love for God. They commit to worshipping Him alone, following Him and obeying all of His commandments. They enjoy His blessings.

- **Rebellion.** But over time, they again REBEL and fall away from God into sin - idolatry, adultery, and disobedience. God sends his prophets to warn of coming consequences and when they refuse to listen to the prophets and His Holy Word, they fall into the hands of their enemies and suffer oppression. The cycle begins again.

In Chapter 9, the Israelites, after listening to Ezra read and proclaim the Word of God aloud, remembered His providential care and all the wonders He performed for them. They were brokenhearted over their sinfulness, depravity, and unfaithfulness to God. They praised God and thanked Him for His faithfulness. They repented of being "stiff-necked" and "not obeying the commandments." In this next study, covering both Chapters 10 and 11 from the Book of Nehemiah, we follow the broken-hearted people as they sign a new covenant - agreement with God promising to follow Him in everything.

Chapter Eleven Questions

1. ***NEHEMIAN 10.*** In preparation for this study, please read Nehemiah 10: 1 – 39 and **circle** all the promises the people make in the covenant (especially in v. 30-37). Share what caught your attention in these verses.

Nehemiah 10: 1 – 32

Upon the sealed document are the names of Nehemiah the governor, son of Hacaliah,
and Zedekiah; 2 Seraiah, Azariah, Jeremiah, 3 Pashhur, Amariah, Malchijah, 4 Hattush,
Shebaniah, Malluch, 5 Harim, Meremoth, Obadiah, 6 Daniel, Ginnethon, Baruch, 7
Meshullam, Abijah, Mijamin, 8 Maaziah, Bilgai, Shemaiah; these are the priests. 9 And
the Levites: Jeshua son of Azaniah, Binnui of the sons of Henadad, Kadmiel; 10 and
their associates, Shebaniah, Hodiah, Kelita, Pelaiah, Hanan, 11 Mica, Rehob, Hashabiah,
12 Zaccur, Sherebiah, Shebaniah, 13 Hodiah, Bani, Beninu. 14 The leaders of the people:
Parosh, Pahath-moab, Elam, Zattu, Bani, 15 Bunni, Azgad, Bebai, 16 Adonijah, Bigvai,
Adin, 17 Ater, Hezekiah, Azzur, 18 Hodiah, Hashum, Bezai, 19 Hariph, Anathoth, Nebai,
20 Magpiash, Meshullam, Hezir, 21 Meshezabel, Zadok, Jaddua, 22 Pelatiah, Hanan,
Anaiah, 23 Hoshea, Hananiah, Hasshub, 24 Hallohesh, Pilha, Shobek, 25 Rehum,
Hashabnah, Maaseiah, 26 Ahiah, Hanan, Anan, 27 Malluch, Harim, and Baanah.

28The rest of the people, the priests, the Levites, the gatekeepers, the singers, the temple
servants, and all who have separated themselves from the peoples of the lands to
adhere to the law of God, their wives, their sons, their daughters, all who have
knowledge and understanding, 29 join with their kin, their nobles, and enter into a curse
and an oath to walk in God's law, which was given by Moses the servant of God, and
to observe and do all the commandments of the Lord our Lord and his ordinances and
his statutes. 30 We will not give our daughters to the peoples of the land or take their
daughters for our sons; 31 and if the peoples of the land bring in merchandise or any
grain on the Sabbath day to sell, we will not buy it from them on the Sabbath or on a
holy day; and we will forego the crops of the seventh year and the exaction of every
debt.

32 We also lay on ourselves the obligation to charge ourselves yearly one-third of a shekel for the service of the house of our God: 33 for the rows of bread, the regular grain offering, the regular burnt offering, the Sabbaths, the new moons, the appointed festivals, the sacred donations, and the sin offerings to make atonement for Israel, and for all the work of the house of our God. 34 We have also cast lots among the priests, the Levites, and the people, for the wood offering, to bring it into the house of our God, by ancestral houses, at appointed times, year by year, to burn on the altar of the Lord our God, as it is written in the law.

35 We obligate ourselves to bring the first fruits of our soil and the first fruits of all fruit of every tree, year by year, to the house of the Lord; 36 also to bring to the house of our God, to the priests who minister in the house of our God, the firstborn of our sons and of our livestock, as it is written in the law, and the firstlings of our herds and of our flocks; 37 and to bring the first of our dough, and our contributions, the fruit of every tree, the wine and the oil, to the priests, to the chambers of the house of our God; and to bring to the Levites the tithes from our soil, for it is the Levites who collect the tithes in all our rural towns.

38And the priest, the descendant of Aaron, shall be with the Levites when the Levites receive the tithes; and the Levites shall bring up a tithe of the tithes to the house of our God, to the chambers of the storehouse. 39 For the people of Israel and the sons of Levi shall bring the contribution of grain, wine, and oil to the storerooms where the vessels of the sanctuary are, and where the priests that minister, and the gatekeepers and the singers are. We will not neglect the house of our God.

2. ***THE SIGNERS.*** Who signed the sealed document or covenant (v. 1, 9, 14)?

3. ***AN OATH OR CURSE.*** What type of agreement did the Israelites bind themselves to follow (v. 28-29)?

❖Ponderings

a. Why do you think all of the names were listed on the agreement (v. 1-27)? (Note: a very similar list was recorded in Chapter 8.)

b. Why would they make an agreement in writing and then sign it (v. 29)?

4. ***THE SPECIFICS.*** List the specifics of their covenant agreement with God from Chapter 10 (e.g., the Sabbath, the House of God, Marriage, etc.).

Nehemiah 10	Promise to Obey	Mosaic Law
v. 30		Deut. 7: 1-4
v. 31		Deut. 15:1
v. 32		Ex. 30: 11-16
v. 34		Lev. 6: 12-13
v. 35		Deut. 26: 1-3
v. 36		Deut. 12: 6
v. 37		Lev. 27: 30

5. ***FINAL COMMITMENT.*** What were the final words of the covenant (v. 39)?

❖Ponderings

a. How are the focal points of the covenant still important to God today?

b. What agreements are you making with the Lord as a result of reading Nehemiah and the Word of God in this study?

The Covenant and Offerings

The Israelites signed a "curse and oath" covenant agreement "to walk in God's law. "This meant that they could expect a blessing for obedience, or a curse or correction from God if they did not follow through on obeying His Law. They knew what had happened to them as a nation when they walked away in the past. This was a public agreement and in writing so that all who attended would be held responsible for keeping the agreement with God and before each other. They knew that there would be great blessings if the kept it according to Deuteronomy 28: 1- 13:

> "If you will only obey the Lord your God, by diligently observing all his commandments that I am commanding you today, the Lord your God will set you high above all the nations of the earth; 2 all these blessings shall come upon you and overtake you, if you obey the Lord your God. 3 Blessed shall you be in the city, and blessed shall you be in the field. 4 Blessed shall be the fruit of your womb, the fruit of your ground, and the fruit of your livestock, both the increase of your cattle and the issue of your flock. 5 Blessed shall be your basket and your kneading bowl. 6 Blessed shall you be when you come in, and blessed shall you be when you go out. 7 The Lord will cause your enemies who rise against you to be defeated before you; they shall come out against you one way, and flee before you seven ways. 8 The Lord will command the blessing upon you in your barns, and in all that you undertake; he will bless you in the land that the Lord your God is giving you. 9 The Lord will establish you as his holy people, as he has sworn to you, if you keep the commandments of the Lord your God and w
> walk in his ways.

> 10 All the peoples of the earth shall see that you are called by the name of the Lord, and they shall be afraid of you. 11 The Lord will make you abound in prosperity, in the fruit of your womb, in the fruit of your livestock, and in the fruit of your ground in the land that the Lord swore to your ancestors to give you. 12 The Lord will open for you his rich storehouse, the heavens, to give the rain of your land in its season and to bless all your undertakings. You will lend to many nations, but you will not borrow. 13 The Lord will make you the head, and not the tail; you shall be only at the top, and not at the bottom—if you obey the commandments of the Lord your God, which I am commanding you today, by diligently observing them..."

On the other hand, they would expect curses for disobedience, according to **Deuteronomy 28: 15-45:**

> "But if you will not obey the Lord your God by diligently observing all his commandments and decrees, which I am commanding you today, then all these curses shall come upon you and overtake you: 16 Cursed shall you be in the city, and cursed shall you be in the field. 17 Cursed shall be your basket and your kneading bowl. 18 Cursed shall be the fruit of your womb, the fruit of your ground, the increase of your cattle and the issue of your flock. 19 Cursed shall you be when you come in, and cursed shall you be when you go out. 20 The Lord will send upon you disaster, panic, and frustration in everything you attempt to do, until you are destroyed and perish quickly, on account of the evil of your deeds, because you have forsaken me. 21 The Lord will make the pestilence cling to you until it has consumed you off the land that you are entering to possess. 22 The Lord will afflict you with consumption, fever, inflammation, with fiery heat and drought, and with blight and mildew; they shall pursue you until you perish. 23 The sky over your head shall be bronze, and the earth under you iron. 24 The Lord will change the rain of your land into powder, and only dust shall come down upon you from the sky until you are destroyed. 25The Lord will cause you to be defeated before your enemies; you shall go out against them one way and flee before them seven ways. You shall become an object of horror to all the kingdoms of the earth... 30 ...You shall build a house, but not live in it. You shall plant a vineyard, but not enjoy its fruit. 31 ... Your sheep shall be given to your enemies, without anyone to help you. 32 Your sons and daughters shall be given to another people, while you look on; you will strain your eyes looking for them all day but be powerless to do anything. 33 A people whom you do not know shall eat up the fruit of your ground and of all your labors; you shall be continually abused and crushed, 34 and driven mad by the sight that your eyes shall see.

"You shall become an object of horror, a proverb, and a byword among all the peoples where the Lord will lead you…[39] You shall plant vineyards and dress them, but you shall neither drink the wine nor gather the grapes, for the worm shall eat them. [40] You shall have olive trees throughout all your territory, but you shall not anoint yourself with the oil, for your olives shall drop off. [41] You shall have sons and daughters, but they shall not remain yours, for they shall go into captivity... [44] They shall lend to you but you shall not lend to them; they shall be the head and you shall be the tail…[45] All these curses shall come upon you, pursuing and overtaking you until you are destroyed, because you did not obey the Lord your God, by observing the commandments and the decrees that he commanded you."

The parents promised not to "give their daughters to the peoples of the land" because in pagan marriages, the sons or daughters would learn to practice pagan rituals such as worshipping reproductive organs, promiscuity in pagan temples with resulting spread of disease, and offering their children in the fire sacrifices to the gods, all of which would lead to a turning away from the living God in worship of idols. They promised not to buy or sell on the Sabbath because God had commanded them to keep the Sabbath holy. They promised to offer sin offerings and atonement for Israel as well to offer tithe and first fruits of their farming (e.g., grain, wine, and oil) and any increase to keep the work of the House of God going. They promised to keep the law of the seventh day and the seventh year, which God had commanded so they would rest their bodies and their soil.

In hard times and in good times, the people promised to give God their best—to pay their tithes to support the temple—to honor the Sabbath by not buying or selling, and to uphold a religious marriage among their people so the next generation would not fall into idolatry again. In all this, they showed their commitment to serve God and that everything they owned belonged to Him.

6. ***<u>MOVING INTO THE CITY.</u>*** Once the walls and gates were built and the covenant was signed, it was time to repopulate their city. Please read Nehemiah 11: 1 – 35 and **<u>circle</u>** all reference to the numbers or people as well as the vocations or jobs for those who moved into the city of Jerusalem. Share what caught your attention in these verses.

Nehemiah 11: 1 – 35

Now the leaders of the people lived in Jerusalem; and the rest of the people cast lots to
bring one out of ten to live in the holy city Jerusalem, while nine-tenths remained in the
other towns. 2 And the people blessed all those who willingly offered to live in Jerusalem. 3
These are the leaders of the province who lived in Jerusalem; but in the towns of Judah all
lived on their property in their towns: Israel, the priests, the Levites, the temple servants,
and the descendants of Solomon's servants. 4 And in Jerusalem lived some of the Judahites
and of the Benjaminites. Of the Judahites: Athaiah son of Uzziah son of Zechariah son of
Amariah son of Shephatiah son of Mahalalel, of the descendants of Perez; 5 and Maaseiah
son of Baruch son of Col-hozeh son of Hazaiah son of Adaiah son of Joiarib son of
Zechariah son of the Shilonite. 6 All the descendants of Perez who lived in Jerusalem were
four hundred sixty-eight valiant warriors.

7 And these are the Benjaminites: Sallu son of Meshullam son of Joed son of Pedaiah son of
Kolaiah son of Maaseiah son of Ithiel son of Jeshaiah. 8 And his brothers Gabbai, Sallai:
nine hundred twenty-eight. 9 Joel son of Zichri was their overseer; and Judah son of
Hassenuah was second in charge of the city.

10Of the priests: Jedaiah son of Joiarib, Jachin, 11 Seraiah son of Hilkiah son of Meshullam
son of Zadok son of Meraioth son of Ahitub, officer of the house of God, 12 and their
associates who did the work of the house, eight hundred twenty-two; and Adaiah son of
Jeroham son of Pelaliah son of Amzi son of Zechariah son of Pashhur son of Malchijah, 13
and his associates, heads of ancestral houses, two hundred forty-two; and Amashsai son
of Azarel son of Ahzai son of Meshillemoth son of Immer, 14 and their associates, valiant
warriors, one hundred twenty-eight; their overseer was Zabdiel son of Haggedolim.

15And of the Levites: Shemaiah son of Hasshub son of Azrikam son of Hashabiah son of
Bunni; 16 and Shabbethai and Jozabad, of the leaders of the Levites, who were over the
outside work of the house of God; 17 and Mattaniah son of Mica son of Zabdi son of
Asaph, who was the leader to begin the thanksgiving in prayer, and Bakbukiah, the
second among his associates; and Abda son of Shammua son of Galal son of Jeduthun. 18
All the Levites in the holy city were two hundred eighty-four.

19 The gatekeepers, Akkub, Talmon and their associates, who kept watch at the gates, were
one hundred seventy-two. 20 And the rest of Israel, and of the priests and the Levites, were
in all the towns of Judah, all of them in their inheritance. 21 But the temple servants lived
on Ophel; and Ziha and Gishpa were over the temple servants.

[22] The overseer of the Levites in Jerusalem was Uzzi son of Bani son of Hashabiah son of Mattaniah son of Mica, of the descendants of Asaph, the singers, in charge of the work of the house of God. [23] For there was a command from the king concerning them, and a settled provision for the singers, as was required every day. [24] And Pethahiah son of Meshezabel, of the descendants of Zerah son of Judah, was at the king's hand in all matters concerning the people.

[25] And as for the villages, with their fields, some of the people of Judah lived in Kiriath-arba and its villages, and in Dibon and its villages, and in Jekabzeel and its villages, [26] and in Jeshua and in Moladah and Beth-pelet, [27] in Hazar-shual, in Beer-sheba and its villages, [28] in Ziklag, in Meconah and its villages, [29] in En-rimmon, in Zorah, in Jarmuth, [30] Zanoah, Adullam, and their villages, Lachish and its fields, and Azekah and its villages. So they camped from Beer-sheba to the valley of Hinnom. [31] The people of Benjamin also lived from Geba onward, at Michmash, Aija, Bethel and its villages, [32] Anathoth, Nob, Ananiah, [33] Hazor, Ramah, Gittaim, [34] Hadid, Zeboim, Neballat, [35] Lod, and Ono, the valley of artisans. [36] And certain divisions of the Levites in Judah were joined to Benjamin.

7. ***THE MOVE TO JERUSALEM.*** How did the people determine who would move to Jerusalem (v. 1)?

   ❖Ponderings

   a. Why do you think the people were cautious about moving to Jerusalem?

   b. For Nehemiah, why would it be so important to repopulate the city?

   c. Why was it also important for some to live outside the city?

Moving into Jerusalem

Repopulating Jerusalem was essential because this would mean it was actually a city and the more people who lived there, especially the strong men, the safer the city would be. Moving to Jerusalem and giving up farming and friendly neighbors would be a big change for some, yet it was the Holy City to them and that made it glorious. Thus, "the leaders of the people lived in Jerusalem; and the rest of the people cast lots to bring in one out of ten" of those who lived in the surrounding towns. It was a choice for those who wanted to move and "the people blessed all those who willingly offered to live in Jerusalem."

The list of those who moved included leaders of the tribes of Judah and Benjamin, as well as military leaders, Levites and priests, gatekeepers, singers or worshippers (i.e., those who lead worship in the temple) and other servants of the king. The other nine-tenths of the Israelites lived in the surrounding villages kept their fields and villages operating for further support the temple, the city and themselves.

8. ***APPLICATION.*** When Nehemiah was sent to build the physical gates and rebuild the walls, he was also rebuilding spiritual gates and walls. Please ask God where the open gates and broken walls are in your life—spiritual or otherwise— and what you can learn from Nehemiah that will help you rebuild them. Please answer the following questions:

    a. Since **prayer and returning to follow the Word of God** triggered the revival of heart and soul in Nehemiah's time, what will it take in our time to see our nation and families revived? **How should we pray?**

    b. Since **confession of sin and worship** were the focus of prayer that led to revival, what could this mean for us today? How can we "**NOT neglect the House of God**" as the people promised in Nehemiah 10?

    c. Since **greater commitment to read and obey the Word of God, with prayer and confession** lead to revival, what will it take in our time to see our nation and families revived with commitment to follow Christ in everything? **What will YOU pray?**

d. In the Old Testament, the Israelites had to offer sacrifices of the blood of animals to God for their sins. The seriousness of sin and its need for blood sacrifices were on the forefront of the mind of the people of God. Now, as part of the New Testament Church and Body of Christ, we need to keep in the forefront of our minds, the great sacrifice that the blood of Jesus has done for our sins. Daily proclaim 1 Peter 1: 18-21 and Ephesians 1: 3, 7 as thanksgiving to Jesus by replacing every "you," "your," "we," our" and "us" with your name in these verses:

1 Peter 1: 18-21. "You know that [I was] ransomed from the futile ways inherited from [my] ancestors, not with perishable things like silver or gold,
19 but with the precious blood of Christ, like that of a lamb without defect or blemish.
20 He was destined before the foundation of the world, but was revealed at the end of the ages for your sake.
21 Through him [I] have come to trust in God, who raised him from the dead and gave him glory, so that [my] faith and hope are set on God.

Ephesians 1: 3, 7. Blessed be the God and Father of our Lord Jesus Christ, who has blessed [me] in Christ with every spiritual blessing in the heavenly places,
7In him I have redemption through his blood, the forgiveness of our trespasses, according to the riches of his grace that he lavished on [me].

e. God desired that the city of Jerusalem would be **strong**—with strong walls, sturdy gates, and holy people who were willing to defend their faith and their city. God asks the same of us in rebuilding our spiritual gates and broken walls. We are called to build the sturdy structures of strong spiritual life and to **defend** our faith against immoral and worldly ways. Read the following verses and describe what meaning they add on how we can **stay strong and defend** our faith.

1 Corinthian 15: 58. Therefore, my beloved, be steadfast, immovable, always excelling in the work of the Lord, because you know that in the Lord your labor is not in vain.

2 Corinthians 6: 14-16. Do not be mismatched with unbelievers. For what partnership is there between righteousness and lawlessness? Or what fellowship is there between light and darkness? 15 What agreement does Christ have with Beliar*? Or what does a believer share with an unbeliever? 16 What agreement has the temple of God with idols? For we are the temple of the living God.

* **Note.** Beliar was another name for Satan.

1 Peter 3: 14-16. Do not be intimidated, [15] but in your hearts, sanctify Christ as Lord. Always be ready to make your defense to anyone who demands from you an accounting for the hope that is in you; [16] yet do it with gentleness and reverence…

Jude 3, 20-25. Beloved, while eagerly preparing to write to you about the salvation we share, I find it necessary to write and appeal to you to contend for the faith that was once for all entrusted to the saints...[20] But you, beloved, build yourselves up on your most holy faith; pray in the Holy Spirit; [21] keep yourselves in the love of God; look forward to the mercy of our Lord Jesus Christ that leads to eternal life. [22] And have mercy on some who are wavering; [23] save others by snatching them out of the fire; and have mercy on still others with fear, hating even the tunic defiled by their bodies. [24] Now to him who is able to keep you from falling, and to make you stand without blemish in the presence of his glory with rejoicing, [25] to the only God our Savior, through Jesus Christ our Lord, be glory, majesty, power, and authority, before all time and now and forever. Amen

9. ***PERSONAL PRAYER RESPONSE.*** Nehemiah has taught us that no brokenness is beyond God's hand of healing when we come to Him in prayer and faith. God wants to lead YOU in rebuilding broken gates and bringing a revival of faith, prayer, repentance and Scripture to those around you. Try to focus on the broken gates of your life, your family, and your nation. Nehemiah models how to pray and intercede to our **Awesome** God summarized in the acronym ABCD (starting with D):

- **Declare** God's greatness and faithfulness with praises and Scripture,

- **Confess** our sins and those of our nation and families,

- **Believe** God and His Holy Word, and

- **Ask** for what you need and use Scripture, when possible.

PREPARE FOR PRAYER

1) Write down your concerns.

MY CONCERNS AND/OR OPEN GATES WHERE I NEED JOY INCLUDE:

2) Listen to the Holy Spirit who will guide you in prayer.

3) Recall God's greatness using scripture (see the Appendix for help with *Scriptures for Declaring God's Greatness* and *Praying with Confidence*).

4) Pray and write a summary of your prayer in the space on the next page.

MY INTERCESSORY PRAYER BASED ON NEHEMIAH 10- 11

- **D**eclare God's Greatness (with Scripture)

- **C**onfess the sins of your nation, your family, and yourself with the same passion as if indeed they all belonged to you.

- **B**elieve the truth of God's Word and His Faithfulness by recalling His blessings and the promises in Scripture (use those verses in prayer).

- **A**sk God for the needs He brings to mind. (Let the Holy Spirit lead you in prayer.)

12

THE CELEBRATION

Connection Question

What do you and your family do to really CELEBRATE something? What religious holiday does your family celebrate with great joy?

The Levites Dedicate the Wall of Jerusalemxxxviii
St. Takla.Org
Nehemiah 12: 27-30

Chapter Twelve - The Celebration

The Covenant and the Move to Jerusalem

In our last study, we joined the Israelites as they signed a public "curse and oath" covenant agreement "to walk in God's law, "which meant they could expect a blessing for obedience or a curse from God if they did not follow through. In hard times and in good times, the people promised to give God their best, to pay their tithes to support the temple, to honor the Sabbath by not buying or selling, and to uphold a Hebrew marriage among their children so the next generation would not fall into idolatry again. Thus, they showed their commitment to serve God believing that everything they owned belonged to Him.

Next, they focused on repopulating Jerusalem because this would make it a true city and create a good defense. Moving to Jerusalem and giving up farming and friendly neighbors would be a big change for some, yet it was the Holy City to them and that made it glorious. Today, we will read Nehemiah 12 and join the people in the dedication ceremony of their city walls and gates to God, and witness their prayer for God's protection. It will be quite a celebration!

Chapter Twelve Questions

1. ***NEHEMIAH 12.*** In preparation for this study, please read Nehemiah 12 and **circle** all the people did to celebrate the completion of the Walls (especially in v. 27-77). Share what caught your attention in these verses.

Nehemiah 12: 1 – 47

These are the priests and the Levites who came up with Zerubbabel son of Shealtiel, and
Jeshua: Seraiah, Jeremiah, Ezra, 2 Amariah, Malluch, Hattush, 3 Shecaniah, Rehum,
Meremoth, 4 Iddo, Ginnethoi, Abijah, 5 Mijamin, Maadiah, Bilgah, 6 Shemaiah, Joiarib,
Jedaiah, 7 Sallu, Amok, Hilkiah, Jedaiah. These were the leaders of the priests and of their
associates in the days of Jeshua.

8 And the Levites: Jeshua, Binnui, Kadmiel, Sherebiah, Judah, and Mattaniah, who with his
associates was in charge of the songs of thanksgiving. 9 And Bakbukiah and Unno their
associates stood opposite them in the service. 10 Jeshua was the father of Joiakim, Joiakim
the father of Eliashib, Eliashib the father of Joiada, 11 Joiada the father of Jonathan, and
Jonathan the father of Jaddua.

12 In the days of Joiakim the priests, heads of ancestral houses, were: of Seraiah, Meraiah; of
Jeremiah, Hananiah; 13 of Ezra, Meshullam; of Amariah, Jehohanan; 14 of Malluchi,
Jonathan; of Shebaniah, Joseph; 15 of Harim, Adna; of Meraioth, Helkai; 16 of Iddo,
Zechariah; of Ginnethon, Meshullam; 17 of Abijah, Zichri; of Miniamin, of Moadiah, Piltai;
18 of Bilgah, Shammua; of Shemaiah, Jehonathan; 19 of Joiarib, Mattenai; of Jedaiah, Uzzi; 20
of Sallai, Kallai; of Amok, Eber; 21 of Hilkiah, Hashabiah; of Jedaiah, Nethanel.

22 As for the Levites, in the days of Eliashib, Joiada, Johanan, and Jaddua, there were
recorded the heads of ancestral houses; also the priests until the reign of Darius the
Persian. 23 The Levites, heads of ancestral houses, were recorded in the Book of the Annals
until the days of Johanan son of Eliashib. 24 And the leaders of the Levites: Hashabiah,
Sherebiah, and Jeshua son of Kadmiel, with their associates over against them, to praise
and to give thanks, according to the commandment of David the man of God, section
opposite to section. 25 Mattaniah, Bakbukiah, Obadiah, Meshullam, Talmon, and Akkub
were gatekeepers standing guard at the storehouses of the gates. 26 These were in the days
of Joiakim son of Jeshua son of Jozadak, and in the days of the governor Nehemiah and of
the priest Ezra, the scribe.

Dedication of the Wall of Jerusalem

27 Now at the dedication of the wall of Jerusalem they sought out the Levites in all their
places, to bring them to Jerusalem to celebrate the dedication with rejoicing, with
thanksgivings and with singing, with cymbals, harps, and lyres. 28 The companies of the
singers gathered together from the circuit around Jerusalem and from the villages of the
Netophathites; 29 also from Beth-gilgal and from the region of Geba and Azmaveth; for the
singers had built for themselves villages around Jerusalem. 30 And the priests and the
Levites purified themselves; and they purified the people and the gates and the wall.

31Then I brought the leaders of Judah up onto the wall, and appointed two great
companies that gave thanks and went in procession. One went to the right on the wall to
the Dung Gate; 32 and after them went Hoshaiah and half the officials of Judah, 33 and
Azariah, Ezra, Meshullam, 34 Judah, Benjamin, Shemaiah, and Jeremiah, 35 and some of the
young priests with trumpets: Zechariah son of Jonathan son of Shemaiah son of Mattaniah
son of Micaiah son of Zaccur son of Asaph; 36 and his kindred, Shemaiah, Azarel, Milalai,
Gilalai, Maai, Nethanel, Judah, and Hanani, with the musical instruments of David the
man of God; and the scribe Ezra went in front of them. 37 At the Fountain Gate, in front of
them, they went straight up by the stairs of the city of David, at the ascent of the wall,
above the house of David, to the Water Gate on the east.

38 The other company of those who gave thanks went to the left, and I followed them with
half of the people on the wall, above the Tower of the Ovens, to the Broad Wall, 39 and
above the Gate of Ephraim, and by the Old Gate, and by the Fish Gate and the Tower of
Hananel and the Tower of the Hundred, to the Sheep Gate; and they came to a halt at the
Gate of the Guard. 40 So both companies of those who gave thanks stood in the house of
God, and I and half of the officials with me; 41 and the priests Eliakim, Maaseiah,
Miniamin, Micaiah, Elioenai, Zechariah, and Hananiah, with trumpets; 42 and Maaseiah,
Shemaiah, Eleazar, Uzzi, Jehohanan, Malchijah, Elam, and Ezer. And the singers sang with
Jezrahiah as their leader. 43 They offered great sacrifices that day and rejoiced, for God had
made them rejoice with great joy; the women and children also rejoiced. The joy of
Jerusalem was heard far away.

Appointments to Temple Responsibilities

44On that day men were appointed over the chambers for the stores, the contributions, the
first fruits, and the tithes, to gather into them the portions required by the law for the
priests and for the Levites from the fields belonging to the towns; for Judah rejoiced over
the priests and the Levites who ministered. 45 They performed the service of their God and
the service of purification, as did the singers and the gatekeepers, according to the
command of David and his son Solomon. 46 For in the days of David and Asaph long ago
there was a leader of the singers, and there were songs of praise and thanksgiving to God.
47 In the days of Zerubbabel and in the days of Nehemiah all Israel gave the daily portions
for the singers and the gatekeepers. They set apart that which was for the Levites; and the
Levites set apart that which was for the descendants of Aaron.

2. ***<u>DEDICATING THE WALL</u>*** <u>(12: 27-31).</u> What kind of prayer meeting was going on at the dedication of the wall (v. 27-29)?

❖Ponderings

a. Why is joy an important part of celebrations for God?

b. What did the priests and Levites do first before celebrating and why would they do that (v. 30)?

c. How does thanksgiving to God contribute to joyful celebration?

3. ***THE PROCESSION AND REJOICING.*** Who lead the procession (v. 31-36)?

❖Ponderings

a. How different was this procession from the one Nehemiah did around the city of Jerusalem at night when he first arrived (2: 11-16)?

b. What happened in the House of God (v. 40-47)?

c. Who rejoiced and how loud was it (v. 40-43)?

4. ***TITHE AND OFFERINGS FOR THE TEMPLE.*** What did the people do to show their respect for those who served as spiritual leaders and in various ways in the temple (v. 44, 47)?

❖Ponderings

a. What duties were involved in the ministry of the priests and Levites (v. 45)?

b. Who served in the temple besides the priests and Levites (v. 46)?

Celebration

Chapter 12 opens with more names - but this time the names were those of "priests and Levites who came up [returned] with Zerubbabel... and with Jeshua" over 100 years ago (v. 1). As you might remember, it was Zerubbabel, the high priest, who led the first return from captivity in Babylon to Jerusalem in 538 B.C. Nehemiah is recalling the history and heroes listed in the public record representing those in spiritual leadership who sacrificed much in returning to Jerusalem. In v. 12 to 21, he lists the priests in the day of the High Priest Joachim and in v. 21- 26, he lists the Levites during the reign of Darius the Persian (possibly an added historical note added to the original text and referring to the King Darius Codomannus, the last king of the Persian monarchy, whom Alexander the Great conquered).

Not that the people had moved into Jerusalem, and returned to worship, observing holy feast days and obeying God's laws, it was time to dedicate the walls and the city to God. The people would show their dedication and implore His presence and blessing. The priests purified themselves and the people—in a national purification—before coming into the presence of God. It was required for them to remove their sins and defilement before worship. **Psalm 24: 3-6** reminds us why this is important for all:

> "Who shall ascend the hill of the Lord? And who shall stand in his holy place? [4] Those who have clean hands and pure hearts, who do not lift up their souls to what is false, and do not swear deceitfully. [5] They will receive blessing from the Lord, and vindication from the God of their salvation. [6] Such is the company of those who seek him, who seek the face of the God of Jacob."

Following the dedication ceremony, the great praise meeting began. The choirs led the people in praise and worship, with thanksgiving, singing and gladness, sounding cymbals and playing all kinds of stringed instruments and harps. They processed around the walls in the dedication ceremony, possibly inspired by Joshua 6: 1-7 (when God told him in an insurmountable situation to march around the city walls of Jericho and shout; they did and God caused the walls to fall down and gave them a great victory). The worship, the rejoicing, and the singing, was so loud the neighboring towns heard it!

Finally, they consecrated the things belonging to God, offering them back to God. They opened the storerooms in the temple so they could bring in their offerings and first fruits to the Lord in support of the House of God—the temple and the Levites.

5. ***APPLICATION.*** What do you learn about worshipping God from Nehemiah 12? Consider the following possibilities and circle those that pertain most to you:

   a. I need to spend more time rejoicing before God.

   b. I need to confess my sins and purify myself before I worship.

   c. I need to join others in a praise meeting.

   d. I need to express thanksgiving to God every day and in all things.

   e. I need to march around those walls (sing and worship or pray as I walk) declaring that they belong to God and any spiritual strongholds must come down.

   f. I need to bring my offering, first fruits and support into God's house.

   g. I need to ponder the works of the Lord more in the House of the Lord, and pray **Psalm 48**.

Psalm 48: 9-14. We ponder your steadfast love, O God, in the midst of your
temple. 10 Your name, O God, like your praise, reaches to the ends of the earth.
Your right hand is filled with victory. 11 Let Mount Zion be glad, let the towns
of Judah rejoice because of your judgments. 12 Walk about Zion, go all around
it, count its towers, 13 consider well its ramparts; go through its citadels, that
you may tell the next generation 14 that this is God, our God forever and ever.
He will be our guide forever.

6. ***PERSONAL PRAYER RESPONSE.*** Please write a prayer related to rejoicing, purifying, and taking back territory as we studied in Chapter 12. Consider any broken gates of your life, your family, and your nation. Nehemiah models how to pray and intercede to our God as summarized in the acronym ABCD (starting with D):

    - **Declare** God's greatness and faithfulness with praises and Scripture,

    - **Confess** our sins and those of our nation and families,

    - **Believe** God and His Holy Word, and

    - **Ask** for what you need and use Scripture, when possible.

PREPARE FOR PRAYER

1) Write down your concerns.

MY CONCERNS AND BROKEN WALLS OR OPEN GATES INCLUDE:

2) Listen to the Holy Spirit who will guide you in prayer.

3) Recall God's greatness using scripture (see the Appendix for help with *Scriptures for Declaring God's Greatness* and *Praying with Confidence*).

4) Pray and write a summary of your prayer in the space on the next page.

MY INTERCESSORY PRAYER BASED ON NEHEMIAH 12: 1-47

- **D**eclare God's Greatness (with Scripture)

- **C**onfess the sins of your nation, your family, and yourself with the same passion as if indeed they all belonged to you.

- **B**elieve the truth of God's Word and His Faithfulness by recalling His blessings and the promises in Scripture (use those verses in prayer).

- **A**sk God for the needs He brings to mind. (Let the Holy Spirit lead you in prayer.)

13

FORGETTING TO REMEMBER

Connection Question

Do you know someone who once followed God, but later turned away? What happened to them?

Nehemiah See Merchants and Sellers Selling on the Sabbath[xxxix]
St.Takla.org
Nehemiah 13: 15-18

Chapter Thirteen - Forgetting to Remember

The National Purification, Consecration and Praise Gathering

In our last few studies, we joined the Israelites where they signed a public "curse and oath" covenant agreement "to walk in God's law, "which meant they could expect a blessing for obedience or a curse or correction from God if they did not follow through. In hard times and in good times, the people promised to give God their best, to pay their tithes to support the temple, to honor the Sabbath by not buying or selling, and to uphold a Hebrew marriage among their people so the next generation would not fall into idolatry again. Thus, they showed their commitment to serve God and that declared everything they owned belonged to Him.

In Chapter 11 and 12, the people again showed their dedication as they implored God's presence and blessing in a national purification and praise gathering. They opened the storehouses in the temple so they could bring in their offerings and first fruits to the Lord to support the House of God—the temple and the Levites. The choirs led the people in praise and worship with thanksgiving, singing with cymbals, stringed instruments and harps. They processed around the walls, likely inspired by Joshua 6: 1-7 (when God told him in an insurmountable situation to march around the city walls of Jericho and shout; they did, God caused the walls to fall down and gave a great victory). At this time of rededication and worship, the rejoicing and singing were so loud that the neighboring towns heard it!

After serving as Governor of Jerusalem for 12 years, from 444 to 432 BC, it seems that Nehemiah returned to Babylon to serve or to consult with King Artaxerxes (v. 6). About 10 years later, Nehemiah came back to Jerusalem to find the people had broken their covenant promises to God, as signed in Nehemiah 12. This is where we join Nehemiah today.

Chapter Thirteen Questions

1. ***TIME PASSES.*** In preparation for this study, please read Nehemiah 13 and **circle** all the evil practices and ways the people fell away from God and the promises they signed in Nehemiah 12. Share what caught your attention in these verses.

Nehemiah 13: 1 - 31

On that day, they read from the book of Moses in the hearing of the people; and in it
was found written that no Ammonite or Moabite should ever enter the assembly of
God, 2 because they did not meet the Israelites with bread and water, but hired
Balaam against them to curse them—yet our God turned the curse into a blessing. 3
When the people heard the law, they separated from Israel all those of foreign
descent.

Reforms of Nehemiah

4 Now before this, the priest Eliashib, who was appointed over the chambers of the
house of our God, and who was related to Tobiah, 5 prepared for Tobiah a large
room where they had previously put the grain offering, the frankincense, the
vessels, and the tithes of grain, wine, and oil, which were given by commandment to
the Levites, singers, and gatekeepers, and the contributions for the priests. 6 While
this was taking place I was not in Jerusalem, for in the thirty-second year of King
Artaxerxes of Babylon I went to the king. After some time, I asked leave of the king 7
and returned to Jerusalem. I then discovered the wrong that Eliashib had done on
behalf of Tobiah, preparing a room for him in the courts of the house of God. 8 And I
was very angry, and I threw all the household furniture of Tobiah out of the room. 9
Then I gave orders and they cleansed the chambers, and I brought back the vessels
of the house of God, with the grain offering and the frankincense.

10 I also found out that the portions of the Levites had not been given to them; so that
the Levites and the singers, who had conducted the service, had gone back to their
fields. 11 So I remonstrated with the officials and said, "Why is the house of God
forsaken?" And I gathered them together and set them in their stations. 12 Then all
Judah brought the tithe of the grain, wine, and oil into the storehouses. 13 And I
appointed as treasurers over the storehouses the priest Shelemiah, the scribe Zadok,
and Pedaiah of the Levites, and as their assistant Hanan son of Zaccur son of
Matanzas, for they were considered faithful; and their duty was to distribute to their
associates. 14 Remember me, O my God, concerning this, and do not wipe out my
good deeds that I have done for the house of my God and for his service.

Sabbath Reforms Begun.

15 In those days I saw in Judah people treading wine presses on the Sabbath, and bringing
in heaps of grain and loading them on donkeys; and also, wine, grapes, figs, and all kinds
of burdens, which they brought into Jerusalem on the Sabbath day; and I warned them at
that time against selling food. 16 Tyrians also, who lived in the city, brought in fish and all
kinds of merchandise and sold them on the Sabbath to the people of Judah, and in
Jerusalem. 17 Then I remonstrated with the nobles of Judah and said to them, "What is this
evil thing that you are doing, profaning the Sabbath day? 18 Did not your ancestors act in
this way, and did not our God bring all this disaster on us and on this city? Yet you bring
more wrath on Israel by profaning the Sabbath."

19When it began to be dark at the gates of Jerusalem before the Sabbath, I commanded that
the doors should be shut and gave orders that they should not be opened until after the
Sabbath. And I set some of my servants over the gates, to prevent any burden from being
brought in on the Sabbath day. 20 Then the merchants and sellers of all kinds of
merchandise spent the night outside Jerusalem once or twice. 21 But I warned them and
said to them, "Why do you spend the night in front of the wall? If you do so again, I will
lay hands on you." From that time on they did not come on the Sabbath. 22 And I
commanded the Levites that they should purify themselves and come and guard the
gates, to keep the Sabbath day holy. Remember this also in my favor, O my God, and
spare me according to the greatness of your steadfast love.

23 In those days also I saw Jews who had married women of Ashdod, Ammon, and Moab;
24 and half of their children spoke the language of Ashdod, and they could not speak the
language of Judah, but spoke the language of various peoples. 25 And I contended with
them and cursed them and beat some of them and pulled out their hair; and I made them
take an oath in the name of God, saying, "You shall not give your daughters to their sons,
or take their daughters for your sons or for yourselves. 26 Did not King Solomon of Israel
sin on account of such women? Among the many nations there was no king like him, and
he was beloved by his God, and God made him king over all Israel; nevertheless, foreign
women made even him to sin. 27 Shall we then listen to you and do all this great evil and
act treacherously against our God by marrying foreign women?"

28 And one of the sons of Jihadi, son of the high priest Eliashib, was the son-in-law of
Sanballat the Horonite; I chased him away from me. 29 Remember them, O my God,
because they have defiled the priesthood, the covenant of the priests and the Levites.

30Thus I cleansed them from everything foreign, and I established the duties of the priests
and Levites, each in his work; 31 and I provided for the wood offering, at appointed times,
and for the first fruits. Remember me, O my God, for good.

2. ***HEARING THE WORD OF GOD** (V. 1-3).* What happened when the people heard the Book of Moses read aloud (v. 1-3)?

3. ***DISPLEASED** (V. 4-9).* According to Nehemiah 13: 4-9, what greatly displeased Nehemiah? What law was neglected?

4. ***DISREGARDED** (V. 12-14).* According to Nehemiah 13: 10-14, what commitment was disregarded?

5. ***BROKEN** (V. 14-22).* According to Nehemiah 13: 14-22, what promise to God was broken?

6. ***UPSET** (V. 23-27).* According to Nehemiah 13: 23 -27, what law did the people break that terribly upset Nehemiah (they promised not to do this in 10: 30)?

Notes.

Pulling out another man's hair (v. 24, also translated beard) seems crazy to us, but to lose one's hair and beard at that time in Israel was a sign of disgrace and was compared to the judgment of God falling again on Judah. It showed great consternation to the men of Israel.

Speaking Ashdod (v. 23-27) meant the children were speaking their mother's language— not Hebrew, the language of Judah and the language of temple worship. Solomon's sin of marrying foreign women led to idolatry and this was considered great wickedness.

7. ***THE EXAMPLE** (V. 28-31).* According to Nehemiah 13: 28-31, what example does Nehemiah make of Joiada's son and why did he do this?

Forgotten and Fallen Away

Between Chapter 12 and Chapter 13 of the Book Nehemiah, at least 10 years have passed (see v. 13: 6). [xl] Nehemiah had traveled back to Artaxerxes and the Persian Court, and then returned to Jerusalem in 433 BC only to find the people had fallen into evil practices and sin in his absence. He was deeply grieved on how quickly they left their promises and dedication to serve God in everything.

Nehemiah had no choice but to address their sinful actions. Not only had the people given their children in intermarriage to those in the pagan neighboring towns who did not use the sacred Hebrew language, but even the high priest Eliashib was in alignment with Tobiah, the Ammonite chief. In addition, his grandson married the daughter of Sanballet the Samaritan (v. 28). Because of their intermarriage with pagans, the Israelites also stopped obeying the commandments, especially to keep the Sabbath Day holy. Now they were engaged in business, operated the wine press and farmed on the *Day of Rest*. They also stopped paying tithe to support the temple and the Levites so the Levites had to return to farming to support their families instead of focusing on serving God and His people. In addition, the Israelites stopped revering the temple. The high priest Eliashib (v. 5) had allowed Tobiah to move into the temple storeroom, where the offerings were kept. Thus, Nehemiah exhorted them to stop the mixed marriages to the pagans, the sacrilege of the Sabbath and the disrespect for the Temple.

What caused the people to fall away so quickly? They only heard the Word of God at public gatherings so they were not reminded daily of God's ways. When the high priest aligned himself with pagans and fell away from God, so did the people. Once they started falling on the downward slope of disobedience, they fell headlong further into disobedience. In the entire spiritual cleanup Nehemiah attempted, he prayed: "Remember me, O my God, concerning this, and do not wipe out my good deeds that I have done for the house of my God and for his service." Nehemiah knew the scriptures and the law of God. His prayer was based in the prayers in the psalms and was likely a common prayer. For example, **Psalm 106: 4-5**, says:

> Remember me, O Lord, when you show favor to your people; help me when you deliver them; that I may see the prosperity of your chosen ones, that I may rejoice in the gladness of your nation, that I may glory in your heritage.

Remembrance was a theme throughout the book of Nehemiah. The people had forgotten God, but Nehemiah called on them to remember God's faithfulness and promises. He called on God to remember the promises of His covenant. God remembered, but the people forgot so often.

8. ***THE FINAL PRAYER** (V. 31).* According to Nehemiah 13: 31, what is Nehemiah's final prayer?

❖Ponderings

a. Why do you think Nehemiah kept asking the Lord to remember him?

b. What do you want the Lord to remember most about YOU? List it in the space below.

9. ***APPLICATION.*** When Nehemiah was sent to rebuild the physical gates and walls, he was also rebuilding the spiritual gates and walls of the Israelites. During this study, you too considered rebuilding the spiritual gates and walls in your life, your family and your nation. Where did you find brokenness? What did you ask God to help rebuild?

❖Ponderings

a. The people in Nehemiah quickly gave into sin and disobedience to God. What does this study in the Book of Nehemiah and especially Chapter 13 convey to you about the importance of standing firm in your faith?

b. What do these verses add to your ponderings about standing strong in your faith?

1 Corinthians 10: 9-14. We must not put Christ to the test, as some of them did and were destroyed by serpents [Numbers 21:5+]; 10And do not complain as some of them did [Numbers 14:2]; and were destroyed by the destroyer [Death Angel] [Exodus 14:29]. 11These things happened to them as an example, but they were written down to instruct us, on whom the ends of the ages have come. 12 So if you think you are standing, watch out that you do not fall. 13No testing has overtaken you that is not common to everyone. God is faithful, and he will not let you be tempted beyond your strength, but with the testing he will provide the way out so that you may be able to endure it. 14 Therefore, my dear friends, flee from the worship of idols.

Psalm 119: 11. I treasure your word in my heart so that I might not sin against you.

Jeremiah 17: 5-7. Thus, says the Lord: Cursed are those who trust in mere mortals and make mere flesh their strength, whose hearts turn away from the Lord. 6 They shall be like a shrub in the desert, and shall not see when relief comes. They shall live in the parched places of the wilderness, in an uninhabited salt land. 7 Blessed are those who trust in the Lord, whose trust is the Lord. 8 They shall be like a tree planted by water, sending out its roots by the stream. It shall not fear when heat comes, and its leaves shall stay green; in the year of drought it is not anxious, and it does not cease to bear fruit.

c. The Bible uses many terms for falling away from faith and gives us ideas about what we can do to avoid a FALL. Which of the following cautions are most meaningful to you?

Deuteronomy 8: 13-16 (Forgetting God and what he has done for you): [When your herds and flocks have multiplied, and your silver and gold is multiplied, and all that you have is multiplied, [14] then do not exalt yourself, forgetting the Lord your God, who brought you out of the land of Egypt, out of the house of slavery, [15] who led you through the great and terrible wilderness, an arid wasteland with poisonous snakes and scorpions. He made water flow for you from flint rock, [16] and fed you in the wilderness with manna that your ancestors did not know, to humble you and to test you, and in the end to do you good...

Revelation 2: 4-7 (Forsaking Your First Love). But I have this against you, that you have abandoned the love you had at first. [5] Remember then from what you have fallen; repent, and do the works you did at first. If not, I will come to you and remove your lampstand from its place, unless you repent. [6] Yet this is to your credit: you hate the works of the Nicolaitans, which I also hate. [7] Let anyone who has an ear listen to what the Spirit is saying to the churches. To everyone who conquers, I will give permission to eat from the tree of life that is in the paradise of God.

Galatians 1: 6-8 (Turning Away from the Gospel). I am astonished that you are so quickly deserting the one who called you in the grace of Christ and are turning to a different gospel— [7] not that there is another gospel, but there are some who are confusing you and want to pervert the gospel of Christ. [8] But even if we or an angel from heaven should proclaim to you a gospel contrary to what we proclaimed to you, let that one be accursed!

Hebrews 6: 10-12 (Becoming Lazy in your Christian walk). For God is not unjust; he will not overlook your work and the love that you showed for his sake in serving the saints, as you still do. [11] And we want each one of you to show the same diligence so as to realize the full assurance of hope to the very end, [12] so that you may not become sluggish [lazy], but imitators of those who through faith and patience inherit the promises.

Matthew 5: 13 (Losing Saltiness). You are the salt of the earth; but if salt has lost its taste, how can its saltiness be restored? It is no longer good for anything, but is thrown out and trampled underfoot.

Thessalonians 5: 6-11 (Falling Asleep). So then let us not fall asleep as others
do, but let us keep awake and be sober; 7 for those who sleep, sleep at night,
and those who are drunk get drunk at night. 8 But since we belong to the day,
let us be sober, and put on the breastplate of faith and love, and for a helmet
the hope of salvation. 9 For God has destined us not for wrath but for
obtaining salvation through our Lord Jesus Christ, 10 who died for us, so that
whether we are awake or asleep we may live with him. 11 Therefore encourage
one another and build up each other, as indeed you are doing.

10. ***PERSONAL PRAYER RESPONSE.*** Nehemiah has taught us that no brokenness is beyond healing and change when we come to Him in prayer and faith. Nehemiah models how to pray and intercede to our God summarized in the acronym ABCD (starting with D). Now please write a prayer related to standing FIRM in your faith and healing the brokenness in your life, your family, and your nation. Include any open gates in that need to be closed or healed.

- **Declare** God's greatness and faithfulness with praises and Scripture,

- **Confess** our sins and those of our nation and families,

- **Believe** God and His Holy Word, and

- **Ask** for what you need and use Scripture, when possible.

In the following space, please write a prayer for yourself, your family and your nation using the ABCD themes.

PREPARE FOR PRAYER

1) Write down your concerns.

MY CONCERNS AND/OR OPEN GATES WHERE I NEED JOY INCLUDE:

2) Listen to the Holy Spirit who will guide you in prayer.

3) Recall God's greatness using scripture (see the Appendix for help with *Scriptures for Declaring God's Greatness* and *Praying with Confidence*).

4) Pray and write a summary of your prayer in the space on the next page.

MY INTERCESSORY PRAYER BASED ON NEHEMIAH 13

- **D**eclare God's Greatness (with Scripture)

- **C**onfess the sins of your nation, your family, and yourself with the same passion as if indeed they all belonged to you.

- **B**elieve the truth of God's Word and His Faithfulness by recalling His blessings and the promises in Scripture (use those verses in prayer).

- **A**sk God for the needs He brings to mind. (Let the Holy Spirit lead you in prayer.)

14

THE FINALE

Connection Question

What do you remember most from the Book of Nehemiah?

Nehemiah Commands the People to Shut the Gates on the Sabbath[xli]
St.Takla.Org
Nehemiah 13:19-21

Chapter Fourteen – The Finale

Remembering to Not Forget God

In our last study, we joined Nehemiah as he returned to Jerusalem after being away for a year or more. He had served as Governor in Jerusalem for 12 years, instigated major reforms and then traveled back to visit King Artaxerxes and the Persian Court. Unfortunately, when he returned to Jerusalem, he found the people had fallen away from their dedication to God and were engaging in evil practices.

Nehemiah was terribly grieved because he feared that without God's protection and guidance, the nation could quickly fall into a situation worse than the Babylonian captivity. He set about to address their sinfulness. The people had given their children in pagan marriages so they no longer spoke the sacred Hebrew language. The high priest had aligned himself with Israel's enemies—Eliashib had partnered with Tobiah, the Ammonite chief and his grandson married the daughter of Sanballet. The Israelites stopped keeping the Sabbath Day holy and instead allowed business, operated the wine press and farmed on the Day of Rest. They stopped paying tithe to support the temple so the Levites returned to farming, and they stopped revering the temple because the high priest had allowed Tobiah to move into the temple storage room where the offerings were stored.

The root of the problem was that the people did not REMEMBER who God was and who they were. In the entire spiritual cleanup Nehemiah attempted, he prayed: "Remember me, O my God, concerning this, and do not wipe out my good deeds that I have done for the house of my God and for his service" (v. 14). Nehemiah knew the scriptures and the law of God. His prayer was based in the psalms. For example, **Psalm 106: 4-5**, says: "Remember me, O Lord, when you show favor to your people; help me when you deliver them; that I may see the prosperity of your chosen ones, that I may rejoice in the gladness of your nation, that I may glory in your heritage."

Remembrance was a theme throughout the book of Nehemiah. The people had forgotten God, but Nehemiah called on them to remember God, His faithfulness and His promises. He also called on God to remember His covenant with His people. God always remembered His people, but the people so often forgot Him.

Chapter Fourteen Questions

1. ***JERUSALEM.*** What did you learn about the people and the city of Jerusalem from this study?

Nehemiah and the Importance of Jerusalem

Jerusalem was an important city to the Israelites. At the time of the Old Testament, it was called the City of David or Zion (meaning fortress). It was the political seat of King David, but most importantly it was home of the temple and place where the Israelites worshipped. For that reason, Jerusalem was called the Holy City, and God said (2 Kings 21:4), "In Jerusalem I will put my name." Thus, when the prophets Jeremiah (9: 11) and Ezekiel (see chapters 4-7) warned God's people about disasters to come resulting from their infidelity, they knew it would mean an end of the temple—the center of worship. Even when the destruction came and many of God's people were taken captive to Babylon, the desire to worship in Jerusalem remained in the hearts of the Jewish people.

In Nehemiah 1, we read of Nehemiah's great anguish and prayers for the restoration of Jerusalem. God answered his prayers, made a way for them to take action and the City of Jerusalem was rebuilt relying on great prayers and great labors. Unfortunately, within a few short years, God's people stopped remembering Him, stopped listening to Him and fell into sin and idolatry.

When Jesus began his earthly ministry, we are reminded of the importance of Jerusalem to Him. In Matthew, Mark, Luke, and John, Jesus' ministry moved toward Jerusalem, the place of His Passion, Death and Resurrection. Jesus even spoke of this in **Luke 13: 33-35**:

> "Yet today, tomorrow, and the next day I must be on my way, because it is
> impossible for a prophet to be killed outside of **Jerusalem.'** [34] **Jerusalem, Jerusalem,**
> the city that kills the prophets and stones those who are sent to it! How often have I
> desired to gather your children together as a hen gathers her brood under her wings,
> and you were not willing! [35] See, your house is left to you. And I tell you, you will
> not see me until the time comes when you say, 'Blessed is the one who comes in the
> name of the Lord.'"

Jesus entered Jerusalem as the Messiah, the Son of David (Matthew 21: 1-11). He died for our sins "so that everyone who believes in Him may not perish but may have eternal life" (John 3:16). It was from Jerusalem that this Good News of the Gospel was first preached and then sent out via the apostles and disciples to the entire world. It was in Jerusalem that the Holy Spirit fell at Pentecost. It was in Jerusalem that the first Christian community was launched.

The *Catholic Bible Dictionary* reminds us that the visions of the Old Testament prophets for a glorified and heavenly Jerusalem far exceeds the reality of Jerusalem, restored after the Babylonian captivity and described in the Book of Nehemiah:

> "Thus, we are led to contemplate a greater reality: a heavenly Jerusalem—the true holy city and the capital of God's new creation…The earthly Zion is the model of the celestial height on which the New Jerusalem is built and together with the city, it is a place of glory where the redeemed will gather before the Lord… if they remain faithful to the Word of Christ."[xlii]

2. **THE NEW JERUSALEM.** Read Revelation 3: 7, 10-13 and describe what strikes you about the New Jerusalem and our inheritance in the heavenly city.

   Revelation 3: 7, 10-13. "[7]And to the angel of the church in Philadelphia write: 'These words of the holy one [Jesus], the true one, who has the key of David, who opens and no one will shut, who shuts and no one opens…[10] Because you have kept my word of patient endurance, I will keep you from the hour of trial that is coming on the whole world, to test the inhabitants of the earth. [11] I am coming soon; hold fast to what you have, so that no one may seize your crown. [12] If you conquer, I will make you a pillar in the temple of my God; you will never go out of it. I will write on you the name of my God, and the name of the city of my God, the new Jerusalem that comes down from my God out of heaven, and my own new name. [13] Let anyone who has an ear, listen to what the Spirit is saying to the churches.'

3. **THE HEAVENLY JERUSALEM.** Read Revelation 21: 1-14 and describe what heavenly Jerusalem will look like and who will live there.

Revelation 21: 1-14. 1 Then I saw a new heaven and a new earth; for the first heaven
and the first earth had passed away, and the sea was no more. 2 **And I saw the holy
city, the new Jerusalem, coming down out of heaven from God, prepared as a
bride adorned for her husband;** 3 and I heard a loud voice from the throne saying,
"Behold, the home of God is among mortals. He will dwell with them, and they will
be his peoples, and God himself will be with them; 4 he will wipe away every tear
from their eyes, Death will be no more, mourning and crying and pain will be no
more, for the first things have passed away."

5 And the one who was seated on the throne said, "See, I am making all things new."
Also, he said, "Write this, for these words are trustworthy and true." 6 Then he said
to me, "It is done! I am the Alpha and the Omega, the beginning and the end. To the
thirsty I will give water as a gift from the spring of the water of life. 7 Those who
conquer will inherit these things, and I will be their God and they will be my
children 8 But as for the cowardly, the faithless, the polluted, the murderers, the
fornicators, the sorcerers, the idolaters, and all liars, their place will be in the lake
that burns with fire and sulfur, which is the second death." 9 Then came one of the
seven angels…, "Come, I will show you the Bride, the wife of the Lamb." 10 And in
the Spirit, he carried me away to a great, high mountain, and showed me the holy
city Jerusalem coming down out of heaven from God. 11 It has the glory of God, its
radiance like a most rare jewel, like a jasper, clear as crystal. 12 It had a great, high
wall, with twelve gates, and at the gates twelve angels, and on the gates, are
inscribed the names of the twelve tribes of the Israelites; 13 on the east three gates, on
the north three gates, on the south three gates, and on the west three gates. 14 And
the wall of the city had twelve foundations, and on them the twelve names of the
twelve apostles of the Lamb.

4. ***LESSONS FROM NEHEMIAH.*** Read the next the following chart that summarizes the lessons the Book of Nehemiah. Please circle the lessons most meaningful to you and write in the space provided what you learned from each section.

Lessons from Nehemiah to Help Rebuild Our Lives, Our Families and Our Nation

a. **Be Passionate about God and Your Nation**
   - Nehemiah loved God, his beloved nation Israel, his city Jerusalem and his community.
   - When he heard of the brokenness of Jerusalem, he wept, mourned, fasted and prayed over the condition of his nation and his people for 4 months.
   - **I learned:**

b. **Become a Person of Prayer and Intercession.**
   - Nehemiah was a man of prayer; he prayed constantly and bathed his work and the work of his people in prayer.
   - He demanded nothing but spent his life on his knees, praying about each situation.
   - He sought God's guidance and leadership in everything.
   - He taught us the ABCDs of intercession – 1) Declare God's greatness, 2) Confess the sins of our nation, family and ourselves, 3) Believe God's faithfulness and the truth of His Word, and 4) Ask God praying with the truths and promises in His Holy Word.
   - **I learned:**

c. **Become a Fearless One Who Stands Strong Against Enemies.**

- Nehemiah was dependent on God in prayer.
- He waited for God to open the doors for change.
- He spoke courageously to those in authority.
- He asked the king's help for everything he needed.
- He offered his own provisions to rebuild the wall and run the city.
- **I learned:**

d. **Become a Faithful Worker in the Vocation God Gave You.**

- In the vocation of Cupbearer to the king of Persia, Nehemiah followed his heart to serve God.
- God gave favor and the king depended on him and later appointed him Governor of Israel.
- **I learned:**

e. **Stand up to Evil and Your Enemies Relying on Much Prayer.**
   - Nehemiah stood up to his enemies with prayer. The evil men did everything possible to discourage the people and stop the rebuilding of the walls.
   - He showed us that the Devil's tactics almost always include: "God does not care, God is too small, and God cannot help. Therefore, you must take everything into your own hands. "
   - He stood against fierce enemy attacks—from inside the temple, from the workplace and from friends or colleagues.
   - **I learned:**

f. **Commit to Rebuilding the Physical and Spiritual Walls of Jerusalem.**
   - Nehemiah was determined and committed to getting the job done.
   - He set priorities--putting his mind and heart on finishing the walls and gates.
   - He surveyed the problem, developed a plan and stuck to it.
   - **I learned:**

g. **Become an Encourager for People and Follow the Word of God.**
   - When the derisions from the enemies came, Nehemiah prayed and greatly encouraged his people.
   - He was not surprised by opposition; he prepared his people for it.
   - He kept reminding his people that God was with them and the Joy of the Lord was their strength.
   - He encouraged the people to build with one hand holding a weapon and the other holding a brick.
   - He called people to come along side and build in the City who were not builders by vocation.
   - **I learned:**

h. **Become a "Praiser" and Lead Thanksgiving where you are.**
   - With the priest Ezra, Nehemiah called the people to worship and return to following God in everything.
   - With Ezra, he led the people in spiritual restoration, which started with reading the Word of God—the law of God and then praising the greatness of God, confessing the sins for the nation, families, and peoples, and resolving to follow the Word of God in everything.
   - He called for celebrations of praise and thanksgiving to God.
   - He helped the Israelites return to celebrating the sacred feasts, especially the Feast of Booths/ Tabernacles.
   - When people fell away, he passionately called them back to following God in EVERYTHING.
   - **I learned:**

i. **Survey the Problem and Go Forth with Passion.**
   - Nehemiah knew the sins that caused despair and ruin (i.e., failure to obey God's laws, unholy alliances, not paying tithe, not revering the place of worship, doing business instead of worshipping God on the Sabbath Day). Then he encouraged the people to change their ways.
   - He held onto God's leadership in every instance no matter what obstacles he encountered or what it cost him personally, often giving sacrificially from his own resources.
   - **I learned:**

5. ***APPLICATION.*** When Nehemiah was sent to rebuild the physical walls and gates, he worked hard at restoring the spiritual walls and open gates too. What open gates or broken walls for evil are in your life, your family or your nation—spiritual or otherwise? How is God calling you to repair and rebuild these open gates and broken walls?

   a. How has your life or family resembled the brokenness and discouragement found in Jerusalem?

   b. What hope do you have for the renewal and rebuilding of your family, your nation and your life? What will you do NEXT?

   c. What project have you committed to the Lord that He can help you build or rebuild?

6. ***PERSONAL PRAYER RESPONSE.*** Please write a prayer using any of the verses or related Scriptures from our study of the Book of Nehemiah. Nehemiah has taught us to remember God and Who we are—His precious children and people. He has taught us to pray about everything and stand firm against evil. Nehemiah models how to pray and intercede to our God as summarized in the acronym ABCD (starting with D). Now please write a prayer related to standing strong in your faith and healing the brokenness in your life, your family, and your nation. Include any walls or gates that need rebuilding and follow the four themes for your intercessory prayer:

- **Declare** God's greatness and faithfulness with praises and Scripture,

- **Confess** our sins and those of our nation and families,

- **Believe** God and His Holy Word, and

- **Ask** for what you need and use Scripture, when possible.

In the following space, please write a prayer for yourself, your family and your nation using the ABCD themes.

PREPARE FOR PRAYER

1) Write down your concerns.

MY CONCERNS OR OPEN GATES WHERE I NEED JOY INCLUDE:

2) Listen to the Holy Spirit who will guide you in prayer.

3) Recall God's greatness using scripture (see the Appendix for help with *Scriptures for Declaring God's Greatness* and *Praying with Confidence*).

4) Pray and write a summary of your prayer in the space on the next page.

MY INTERCESSORY PRAYER BASED ON WHAT I LEARNED FROM STUDYING THE BOOK OF NEHEMIAH

- **D**eclare God's Greatness (with Scripture)

- **C**onfess the sins of your nation, your family, and yourself with the same passion as if indeed they all belonged to you.

- **B**elieve the truth of God's Word and His Faithfulness by recalling His blessings and the promises in Scripture (use those verses in prayer).

- **A**sk God for the needs He brings to mind. (Let the Holy Spirit lead you in prayer.)

Appendix A

Declarations and Praises of God's Greatness in Scripture

1 Chronicles 29:11. YOURS O Lord, are the greatness, the power, the glory, the victory, and the majesty; for all that is in the heavens and on the earth is yours; YOURS is the kingdom, O Lord, and you are exalted as head above all.

Daniel 2: 20-23. "Blessed be the name of God from age to age, for wisdom and
power are his. 21 YOU change times and seasons, deposes kings and sets up kings;
YOU give wisdom to the wise and knowledge to those who have understanding. 22
YOU reveal deep and hidden things; YOU know what is in the darkness, and light
dwells with YOU. 23 To you, O God of my ancestors, I give thanks and praise, for
you have given me wisdom and power, and have now revealed to me what I asked
of you..."

Exodus 15: 11. "Who is like you, O Lord ...Who is like you, majestic in holiness, awesome in splendor, doing wonders?

1 Chronicles 16: 27. Honor and majesty are before you; strength and joy are in YOUR place.

2 Chronicles 20: 6. "You are the God in heaven. You rule over all the kingdoms of the nations. In YOUR hand are power and might, so that no one is able to withstand you.

Psalm 8:9. O Lord, our Sovereign, how majestic is your name in all the earth! You have set your glory above the heavens.

Psalm 24:10. Who is this King of glory? The LORD of hosts, YOU are the King of glory.

Psalm 95: 3-7. For the Lord is a great God, and a great King above all gods. 4 In your
hand are the depths of the earth; the heights of the mountains are YOURS also. 5 The
sea is YOURS, for you made it, and the dry land, which YOUR hands have formed.
6 O come, let us worship and bow down, let us kneel before the Lord, our Maker!
7 For YOU are our God, and we are the people of your pasture, and the sheep of your
hand.

Colossians 1:16-18. He [JESUS] is the image of the invisible God, the firstborn of all creation; for in him all things in heaven and on earth were created, things visible and invisible, whether thrones or dominions or rulers or powers—all things have been created through him and for him. He himself is before all things, and in him all things hold together. He is the head of the body, the church; he is the beginning, the firstborn from the dead, so that he might come to have first place in everything.

Hebrews 1:3-4. He [JESUS] is the reflection of God's glory and the exact imprint of God's very being, and he sustains all things by his powerful word. When he had made purification for sins, he sat down at the right hand of the Majesty on high, having become as much superior to angels as the name he has inherited is more excellent than theirs.

Appendix B

Scriptures for Praying with the Word of God

Exodus 14:14. The Lord will fight for you, and you have only to keep still.

Exodus 15:26. He said, … for I am the Lord who heals you."

Psalm 3: 3-6. But you, O Lord, are a shield around me, my glory, and the one who lifts up my head. 4 I cry aloud to the Lord, and he answers me from his holy hill. 5 I lie down and sleep; I wake again, for the Lord sustains me. 6 I am not afraid of ten thousands of people who have set themselves against me all around.

Psalm 16: 7-8, 11. I bless the Lord who gives me counsel; in the night also my heart instructs me. 8 I keep the Lord always before me; because he is at my right hand, I shall not be moved. You show me the path of life. 11 In your presence there is fullness of joy; in your right hand are pleasures forevermore.

Psalm 18: 2. The Lord is my rock, my fortress, and my deliverer, my God, my rock in whom I take refuge, my shield, and the horn of my salvation, my stronghold.

Psalm 23. The Lord is my shepherd, I shall not want. 2He makes me lie down in green pastures; he leads me beside still waters; 3 he restores my soul. He leads me in right paths for his name's sake. 4 Even though I walk through the darkest valley, I fear no evil; for you are with me; your rod and your staff—they comfort me. 5 You prepare a table before me in the presence of my enemies; you anoint my head with oil; my cup overflows. 6 Surely goodness and mercy shall follow me all the days of my life, and I shall dwell in the house of the Lord my whole life long.

Psalm 27: 1-3, 13-14. The Lord is my light and my salvation; whom shall I fear? The Lord is the stronghold of my life; of whom shall I be afraid? 2 When evildoers assail me to devour my flesh—my adversaries and foes—they shall stumble and fall. 3 Though an army encamp against me, my heart shall not fear; though war rise up against me, yet I will be confident. I believe that I shall see the goodness of the Lord in the land of the living. 14 Wait for the Lord; be strong, and let your heart take courage; wait for the Lord!

Psalms 28:7. The Lord is my strength and my shield; in YOU my heart trusts; so I am helped, and my heart exults, and with my song I give thanks to YOU.

Psalm 31: 14-15. But I trust in you, O Lord; I say, "YOU are my God." 15 My times are in your hand; deliver me from the hand of my enemies and persecutors.

Psalm 34: 4-9. I sought the Lord, and he answered me, and delivered me from all my fears. 5 Look to him, and be radiant; so your faces shall never be ashamed. 6 This poor soul cried, and was heard by the Lord, and was saved from every trouble. 7 The angel of the Lord encamps around those who fear him, and delivers them. 8 O taste and see that the Lord is good; happy are those who take refuge in him. 9 O fear the Lord, you his holy ones, for those who fear him have no want...

Psalm 34: 17-19. When the righteous cry for help, the Lord hears, and rescues them from all their troubles. 18 The Lord is near to the brokenhearted, and saves the crushed in spirit. 19 Many are the afflictions of the righteous, but the Lord rescues them from them all.

Psalm 43:5. Why are you cast down, O my soul, and why are you disquieted within me? Hope in God; for I shall again praise him, my help and my God.

Psalm 46: 1-3. God is our refuge and strength, a very present help in trouble. 2 Therefore we will not fear, though the earth should change, though the mountains shake in the heart of the sea; 3 though its waters roar and foam, though the mountains tremble with its tumult.

Psalm 55: 16-17. I call upon God, and the Lord will save me. 17 Evening and morning and at noon I will call and he will hear my voice…22 Cast your burden on the Lord, and he will sustain you; he will never permit the righteous to be moved.

Psalm 68: 35. Awesome is God in his sanctuary, the God of Israel; he gives power and strength to his people.

Psalm 84:11. For the Lord God is a sun and shield; he bestows favor and honor. No good thing does the Lord withhold from those who walk uprightly.

Psalm 94: 19. When the cares of my heart are many, YOUR consolations cheer my soul.

Psalm 118. 6-8. With the Lord on my side I do not fear. What can mortals do to me? 7 The Lord is on my side to help me; I shall look in triumph on those who hate me. 8 It is better to take refuge in the Lord than to put confidence in mortals.

Psalm 144: 1-2. Blessed be the Lord, my rock, who trains my hands for war, and my fingers for battle; 2 my rock and my fortress, my stronghold and my deliverer, my shield, in whom I take refuge, who subdues the peoples under me.

Proverbs 3: 5-6. Trust in the Lord with all your heart and do not rely on your own insight. In all your ways acknowledge him, and he will make straight your paths.

Proverbs 4:20-22. My child, be attentive to my words; incline your ear to my sayings.
[21] Do not let them escape from your sight; keep them within your heart. [22] For they
are life to those who find them, and healing to all their flesh.

Isaiah 38: 16. Those live whom the Lord protects; yours is the life of my spirit. You have given me health and restored my life! (NABRE)

Isaiah 59: 1. See, the Lord's hand is not too short to save, nor his ear too dull to hear.

Habakkuk 3:2. O Lord, I have heard of your renown, and I stand in awe, O Lord, of your work. In our own time revive it; in our own time make it known; in wrath may you remember mercy.

Luke 1:46. And Mary said, "My soul magnifies the Lord, and my spirit rejoices in God my Savior.

Ephesians 1:19-21. May I know, what is the immeasurable greatness of his power for us who believe, according to the working of his great power. God put this power to work in Christ when he raised him from the dead and seated him at his right hand in the heavenly places, far above all rule and authority and power and dominion, and above every name that is named, not only in this age but also in the age to come.

Ephesians 3:14-21. For this reason, I bow my knees before the Father, [15] from whom
every family in heaven and on earth takes its name. [16] I pray that, according to the
riches of his glory, he may grant that you may be strengthened in your inner being
with power through his Spirit, [17] and that Christ may dwell in your hearts through
faith, as you are being rooted and grounded in love. [18] I pray that you may have the
power to comprehend, with all the saints, what is the breadth and length and height
and depth, 19 and to know the love of Chris t that surpasses knowledge, so that you
may be filled with all the fullness of God. [20] Now to him who by the power at work
within us is able to accomplish abundantly far more than all we can ask or imagine,
[21] to him be glory in the church and in Christ Jesus to all generations, forever and
ever. Amen.

Appendix C

Guidelines for Small Groups

This Bible study is designed for use in small groups or for personal reflection, and for RCIA programs, or high school religion classes. As a member of a small group, please try to follow these basic guidelines:

- Prepare in advance by completing the chapter for each session.
- Come to each session ready to contribute to the discussion.
- Keep the focus on the study questions and commentary; avoid discussions on current political events or other side issues that can distract the group from focusing on God's Word.
- Pray daily for members of your group.

Tips for Facilitating a Small Group Study

Each small group needs a leader or facilitator who can foster discussion and keep the group focused on the questions and commentary. A facilitator should:

1. **Welcome.** Welcome each of the participants.

2. **Review.** Go over the basic guidelines for small groups (see previous page).

3. **Pray.** Begin each meeting with thanksgiving and prayer, especially invoking the Holy Spirit to guide the session. (For example, you could pray the Come Holy Spirit Prayer.*)

4. **Read.** Begin by asking someone to read the commentary at the beginning of the chapter. (This study is designed so that each chapter is self-contained and thus, all the information needed for each session is provided in the chapter.) Plan to go through an entire chapter together as a group. Maintain involvement by inviting each member to read a Scripture reading or a commentary section.

5. **Invite.** When you get to each study question, as the facilitator, read each one aloud, pausing so that group members have time to share their answers to each question or pondering.

6. **Encourage** all to participate in answering the questions and in discussion so that no one person monopolizes the session or feels left out.

7. **Focus.** Keep the focus on each question and do not allow the group to be distracted from the questions and commentary. If someone tries to lead the group astray on a subject unrelated to answering a question, simply say, "We can discuss that later--after the meeting, but for now let's stay focused on the question and the Scriptures."

8. **Commentary.** Emphasize the commentary, word studies and notes. This study contains supplementary information from historical sources, the Catechism of the Catholic Church and Catholic scholars.

9. **Follow-up.** Encourage each group member to do the chapter study and answer the questions before coming to the session. It will have a huge impact on the depth of the discussion if everyone has prepared in advance. You might also suggest they review the study covered in the present session a second time after the meeting, and thus, allow the Lord to lead them more deeply into the Word of God.

10. **Prayer.** End each session with prayer. Invite popcorn prayer where each person prays a one-sentence prayer for personal needs and then says, "For this I pray to the Lord." Everyone responds, "Lord, hear our prayer." Then another person pops in a one-sentence prayer and the prayers continues.

    Final Tip for New Facilitators If you want to start a new study group, ask the Lord for his counsel—who He wants you to invite into the group, and if there is someone you should ask to help you get it started. Then the two of you will want to pray together often for each other and for the group members. Remember, Jesus sent the disciples out to minister <u>two-by- two.</u> (Luke 9: 1-6)

The Come Holy Spirit Prayer*

Come Holy Spirit,
fill the hearts of your faithful
and kindle in them the fire of your love.
Send forth your Spirit
and they shall be created.
And You shall renew the face of the earth.

O, God, who by the light of the Holy Spirit,
did instruct the hearts of the faithful,
grant that by the same Holy Spirit
we may be truly wise and ever enjoy His consolations,
Through Christ Our Lord. Amen.

Reference List

Anchor Bible Dictionary, Vol. 2, D-G (1992). (David Noel Freedman, Ed.). New York: Double Day.

Brown, F. (2000, 1994). The Enhanced Brown-Driver-Briggs Hebrew and English Lexicon. With an appendix containing the Biblical Aramaic. Electronic ed. Oak Harbor, WA.

Cameli, Fr. Louis. (2011). The Devil You Don't Know - Recognizing and Resisting Evil in Everyday Life. Notre Dame, IN: Ave Maria Press

Carson, D. A., & Nielson, K. B. (2016). God's Word, Our Story: Learning from the Book of Nehemiah. Wheaten, Ill: Crossway.

Cavins, J., & Christmyer, S. (2015). The Bible Timeline Chart. West Chester, PA: Ascension Press

Davies, G. F. (1999). Berit Olam Studies in Hebrew Narrative & Poetry: Ezra and Nehemiah. Michael Glazier Book, published by The Liturgical Press.

Dowley, T. (2007). *St. Joseph Atlas of the Bible.* Totawa, NJ: Catholic Book Publishing.

Encyclopaedia Iranica. Artaxerxes I. Vol. II, Fasc. 6, pp. 655-656. Retrieved March 4, 2017 from http://www.iranicaonline.org/articles/artaxerxes-i

Fanning, W. (1908). The Catholic Encyclopedia. New York: Robert Appleton Company. Retrieved January 6, 2016 from New Advent:

First, M., (2015). Esther Unmasked: Solving Eleven Mysteries of the Jewish Holidays and Liturgy. New York: Kodesh Press. (Excerpt available at TheTorah.com - A Historical and Contextual Approach: http://thetorah.com/if-achashverosh-is-xerxes-is-esther-his-wife-amestris/)

Gottheil, R., & Meyer, E. (1906). ARTAXERXES I. (surnamed Longimanus—"Long-Hand"). The unedited full-text of the 1906 Jewish Encyclopedia ARTAXERXES I. Retrieved March 4, 2017 from http://www.jewishencyclopedia.com/articles/1827-artaxerxes-i

Hahn, S. (2009). *Catholic Bible Dictionary.* New York: Doubleday.

Hardon, Rev. John A., S. J. (2001). *Modern Catholic Dictionary*. Bardstown, KY: Eternal Life.

Haydock, G. (1811, 2016). Catholic Commentary on Nehemiah. Lexington, KY: First Rate Publishers.

Hebrew Dictionary (Lexicon-Concordance) Key Word Studies (Translations-Definitions-Meanings) retrieved from http://lexiconcordance.com/hebrew/0251.html

Herodotus (1954, 2003). *The Histories.* London: Penguin Books

Knecht, Most Reverend F. J., (1923, 2003). A Practical Commentary on Holy Scripture. Rockford, Il; Tan Books and Publishers, Inc.

Kreeft, P. (2000). Prayer for Beginners, Boston: Ignatius Press.

Lockman Foundation (1998). NAS Exhaustive Concordance of the Bible with Hebrew-Aramaic and Greek Dictionaries. Retrieved from: http://www.lockman.org

McKenzie, Rev. John L., S. J., (1965). *Dictionary of the Bible.* Milwaukee: Bruce Publishing.

Navarre Bible Commentaries (2003). Chronicles—Maccabees Texts and Commentaries [Esther]. New York: Scepter Publishers.

Ryle, H. E. (1901). Ezra and Nehemiah. The Cambridge Bible for schools and colleges commentary. Retrieved September 2 , 2017 from http://onlinebooks.library.upenn.edu/webbin/book/lookupname?key=Ryle%2C%20Herbert%20Edward%2C%201856-1925.

Schehr, T. P. (2007). *The Bible Made Easy (Book-by-Book Introduction).* Cincinnati: St. Anthony Messenger.

St. Augustine. Contra Duas Epistulas Pelagianorum, 1.

Stravinskas, Rev. P. (Editor, 1991). *Catholic Encyclopedia.* Huntington, Indiana: Our Sunday Visitor.

Supple, 2017. In Merriam-Webster.com. Retrieved September 2, 2017 from https://www.merriam-webster.com/dictionary/supple

Van Hoonacker, A. (1911). Book of Nehemiah. In *The Catholic Encyclopedia*. New York: Robert Appleton Company. Retrieved September 2, 2017 from New Advent: http://www.newadvent.org/cathen/10737c.htm

Volkmar, F. (1995). *The City in Ancient Israel.* Sheffield: Sheffield Academic Press.

Zanchettin, L. (2011, January). Be a big picture Intercessor. The Word Among Us magazine. Frederick, MD: the WORD among us press.

Ziotnik, Y. (2012a). Were Jewish Coins Struck on Attached Strips of Flans? Israel Numismatic Research 7 (2012), p. 81-93

Ziotnik, Y. (2012b). Minting of coins in Jerusalem during the Persian and Hellenistic periods. From a lecture dated May 13 2013 to the Israel Numismatic Society members Tel Aviv branch. www.ins.org.il/files/files/mintingofcoinsinJerusalemduringthePersianandHellenisticperiod.pdf

Ziotnik Y. 2011. Alexander Jannaeus coins and their dates http://www.academia.edu/694021/Alexander_Jannaeus_coins_and_their_dates_English

Zodhiates, S. (1992). The Complete Word Study Dictionary New Testament. Chattanooga, TN: AMG Publishers.

Endnotes

[i] http://www.wikigallery.org/wiki/painting_198884/William-Brassey-Hole/Nehemiah-makes-his-petition-to-Artaxerxes

[ii] www.jewishencyclopedia.com; Encyclopaedia Iranica. Artaxerxes I http://www.iranicaonline.org/articles/artaxerxes-i; TheTorah.com - A Historical and Contextual Approach

[iii] St. Takla. Org. http://st-takla.org/Gallery/Bible/Illustrations/Bible-Slides/OT/Nehemiah/Bible-Slides-nehemiah-1253.html

[iv] Van Hoonacker, 10737c, The Catholic Encyclopedia; Cavins & Christmyer, 2015

[v] Hahn, 2009, Catholic Bible Dictionary, p. 645

[vi] Hahn, 2009, The Catholic Encyclopedia, p. 645

[vii] Ryle, 1901

[viii] The Brown-Driver-Briggs. (2000, 1994); Hebrew Dictionary Lectionary-Concordance. http://lexiconcordance.com/hebrew/0251.html

[ix] Hahn, The Catholic Encyclopedia

[x] Zodhiates, 1992, #3069

[xi] Zodhiates, 1992, #430

[xii] Zodhiates, 1992, #410

[xiii] Zodhiates, 1992, #2617

[xiv] http://www.nwadvent.org/cathen/08070a.htm

[xv] https://www.merriam-webster.com/dictionary/supple

[xvi] The three steps are adapted from https://wau.org/resources/article/re_be_a_big_picture_intercessor/

[xvii] Hahn, 2009, The Catholic Encyclopedia; Cavins, Grey, & Christmyer, 2016

[xviii] Kreeft, 2000

[xix] St. Takla.org http://st-takla.org/Gallery/Bible/Illustrations/Bible-its-Story/Bible-Story-05/nehemiah-survays-the-ruins.html

[xx] Esther 4:2; Ryle, 1901,

[xxi] Josephus, Ant. 12:160–236; 2 Maccabees 3:11 and 12:17

[xxii] St. Takla. Org http://st-takla.org/Gallery/Bible/Illustrations/Bible-Slides/OT/Nehemiah/Bible-Slides-nehemiah-1261.html

[xxiii] Dowley (2007); Volkmar, 1995

[xxiv] Hahn, 2009, The Catholic Encyclopedia

[xxv] Hahn, 2009, The Catholic Encyclopedia

[xxvi] http://www.nationalreview.com/article/415757/hell-satan-interview

[xxvii] St.Takla.Org http://st-takla.org/Gallery/Bible/Illustrations/Bible-Slides/OT/Nehemiah/Bible-Slides-nehemiah-1264.html

[xxviii] St.Takla.Org http://st-takla.org/Gallery/Bible/Illustrations/Bible-Slides/OT/Nehemiah/Bible-Slides-nehemiah-1266.html

[xxix] Ziotnik, 2011, 2012a, 2012b

[xxx] St.Takla.Org http://st-takla.org/Gallery/Bible/Illustrations/Bible-Slides/OT/Nehemiah/Bible-Slides-nehemiah-1268.html

[xxxi] Fr. Cameli, 2011

[xxxii] St.Takla.Org http://st-takla.org/Gallery/Bible/Illustrations/Bible-Slides/OT/Nehemiah/Bible-Slides-nehemiah-1272.html

[xxxiii] Carson & Nielson, 2016

[xxxiv] St. Takla.Org http://st-takla.org/Gallery/Bible/Illustrations/Bible-Slides/OT/Nehemiah/Bible-Slides-nehemiah-1277.html

[xxxv] http://www.jewishvirtuallibrary.org/sukkot

[xxxvi] St.Takla.Org http://st-takla.org/Gallery/Bible/Illustrations/Bible-Slides/OT/Nehemiah/Bible-Slides-nehemiah-1275.html

[xxxvii] St.Takla.Org http://st-takla.org/Gallery/Bible/Illustrations/Bible-Slides/OT/Nehemiah/Bible-Slides-nehemiah-1278.html

[xxxviii] St.Takla.Org http://st-takla.org/Gallery/Bible/Illustrations/Bible-Slides/OT/Nehemiah/Bible-Slides-nehemiah-1280.html

[xxxix] St.Takla.Org http://st-takla.org/Gallery/Bible/Illustrations/Bible-Slides/OT/Nehemiah/Bible-Slides-nehemiah-1281.html

[xl] Haydock, Nehemiah 13: 1
[xli] St.Takla.Org http://st-takla.org/Gallery/Bible/Illustrations/Bible-Slides/OT/Nehemiah/Bible-Slides-nehemiah-1282.html

[xlii] Hahn, The Catholic Dictionary, 2009, p. 432

Made in the USA
Lexington, KY
08 February 2018